J.W.FISKE.
N.Y.

J. W. FISKE. N. Y

STABLE

& BARN
Fixtures

While every effort has been made to record accurately
and completely all information contained herein, liability
resulting from any errors or omissions is disclaimed

APOLLO BOOK

5 Schoolhouse Lane

Poughkeepsie, NY 12603

914-462-0040

PREFACE

It is very likely that, at some point or another, each of us has wished for the ability to go back in time, to experience life when it was not necessarily easier, but at least a bit less complicated and pressured. The past has always held a kind of wistful intrigue for us, a longing for those renowned "good old days" of which the worst is now clouded from our view and the best shines forth as a reminder of the way things once were.

Perhaps that is why we are attracted so strongly to things from the past. Antiques, heirlooms, and relics, besides being of monetary value, capture our imagination and interest. Since we cannot go back to the past, they bring a little bit of the past to us.

This volume was created to do just that. A reprint of the original 1910 illustrated catalogue from J.W. Fiske Iron Works in New York City, it features over 750 stable and barn fixtures from this unrivaled manufacturer of decorative metals. It is a rare treat for anyone interested in horses, barns, stables, iron work, antiques, and collectible Americana. It is a kind of visual treasure trove that can be used as an identification guide, a restoration aid, an idea book, a reference in dating objects in photographs and paintings, or for the pure pleasure of reminiscence.

Hitching posts, harness brackets, salt dishes, stall guards, weather vanes, grain measures, locks, and lanterns . . . the charming and unique world of *Stable and Barn Fixtures*. It is my hope that this book will bring the good old days of that world a little closer to you.

Glenn B. Opitz
August, 1987

Illustrated

Catalogue and Price List

... of ...

New and Improved

Iron Stable Fixtures

MANUFACTURED BY

J. W. Fiske Iron Works

39 AND 41 PARK PLACE

NEW YORK

FIG. 1 K

ILLUSTRATING STABLE FITTINGS
Furnished by J. W. FISKE IRON WORKS
39 and 41 Park Place, New York

STABLE OF
MISS HELEN M. GOULD
213 W. 58TH STREET
NEW YORK

YORK & SAWYER, ARCHITECTS
156 5TH AVENUE
NEW YORK

FIG. 2 K

ILLUSTRATING STABLE FITTINGS
Furnished by J. W. FISKE IRON WORKS
39 and 41 Park Place, New York

FISKE'S SANITARY STALL DRAINS ARE IN USE IN THIS STABLE

HUGH ROBERTS, ARCHITECT
1 EXCHANGE PLACE
JERSEY CITY
N. J.

STABLE OF
E. F. C. YOUNG, ESQ.
JERSEY CITY HEIGHTS
N. J.

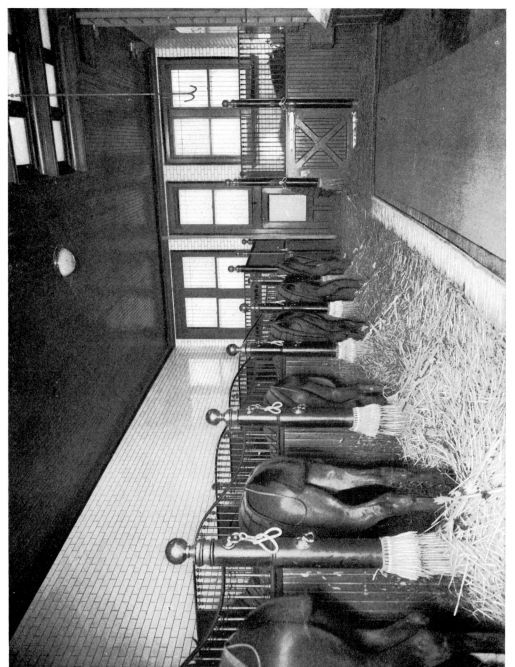

FIG. 3 K

STABLE FITTINGS
Furnished by J. W. FISKE IRON WORKS
39 and 41 Park Place, New York

FISKE'S SANITARY STALL DRAINS ARE IN USE IN THIS STABLE

STABLE OF
FRANK J. GOULD, ESQ.
218 W. 58TH STREET
NEW YORK

JARDINE, KENT & JARDINE, ARCHITECTS
1262 BROADWAY, NEW YORK
WM. HAIGH, BUILDER
NEW YORK

FIG 4 K

ILLUSTRATING STABLE FITTINGS
Furnished by J. W. FISKE IRON WORKS
39 and 41 Park Place, New York

FISKE'S SANITARY STALL DRAINS ARE IN USE IN THIS STABLE

JOHN T. BRAMBLE, ARCHITECT
JOHN WATERS, BUILDER
BALTIMORE, MD.

STABLE OF
NELSON PERRIN, ESQ.
BALTIMORE, MD.

FIG. 5 K

ILLUSTRATING STABLE FITTINGS
Furnished by J. W. FISKE IRON WORKS
39 and 41 Park Place, New York

JOSEPH STILLBERG, ARCHITECT
PITTSBURG, PA.

STABLE OF
T. N. BARNSDALE, ESQ.
PITTSBURG, PA.

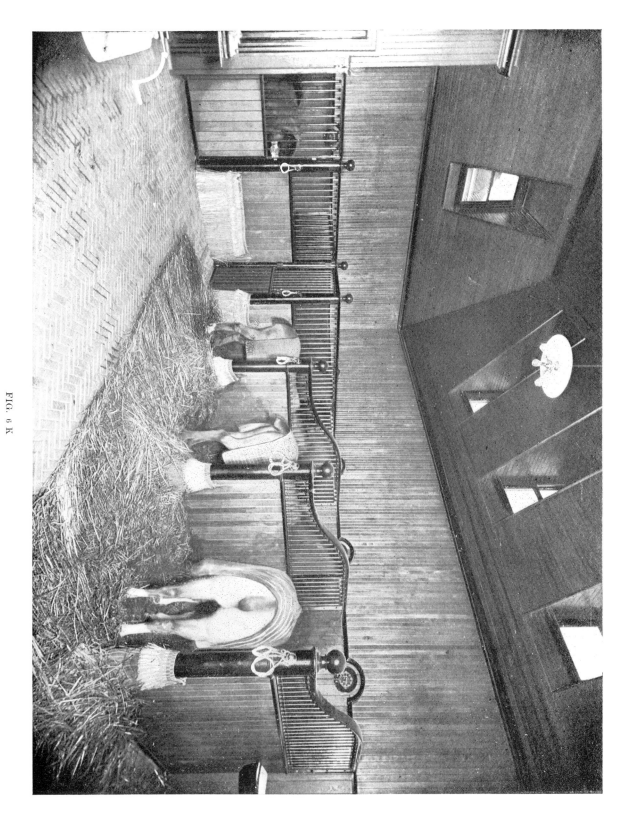

E. B. GUMAER, ARCHITECT
39 CORTLANDT STREET
NEW YORK

FIG. 6 K

ILLUSTRATING STABLE FITTINGS
Furnished by J. W. FISKE IRON WORKS
39 and 41 Park Place, New York

STABLE OF
E. L. YOUNG, ESQ.
JERSEY CITY HEIGHTS, N. J.

Plan Suggesting the Arrangement of Stalls and Fittings.

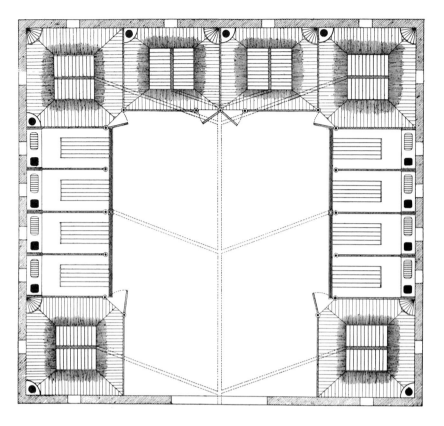

FIG 7 K

Showing the arrangement of six box and eight single stalls, including Fiske's Sanitary Stall
Drains.   Fig. 262 J, Page 74.

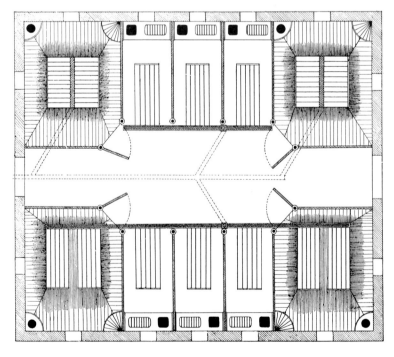

FIG. 8 K

Showing the arrangement of four box and six single stalls, including Fiske's Sanitary Stall
Drains.   Fig. 262 K, Page 74.

Plan Suggesting the Arrangement of Stalls and Fittings.

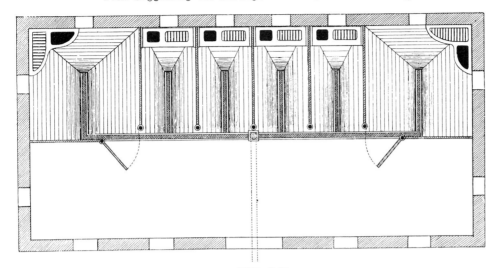

FIG. 9 K

Showing the arrangement of two box and four single stalls, including gutter.

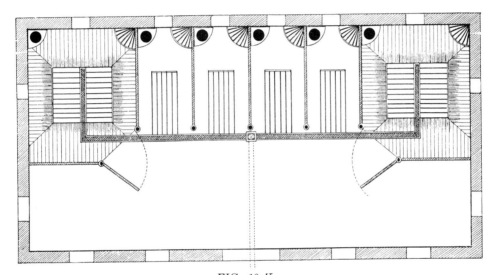

FIG. 10 K

Showing the arrangement of two box and four single stalls, including Fiske's Sanitary Stall Drains. Fig. 263 K, Page 74.

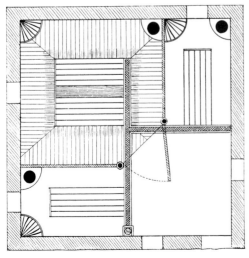

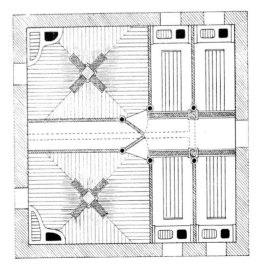

FIG. 11 K

Showing the arrangement of one box and two single stalls, including Fiske's Sanitary Stall Drains. Fig. 263 K, Page 74.

FIG. 12 K

Showing the arrangement of two box and four single stalls, including Fiske's Sanitary Stall Drains. Fig. 263 K, Page 74, for single stalls and trap and gutter branches for box stalls.

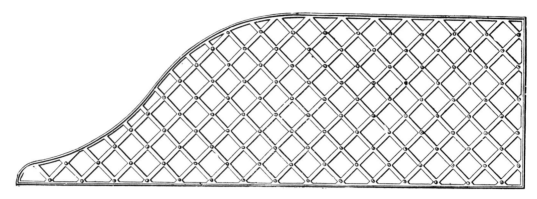

FIG. 13 K

Cast Iron Stall Guard.

Size, 5 feet	long,	2 feet	high, round end, each				$4.00
" 5 "	"	2 " 4 in. "	"	"	"		4.50
" 5 " 6 in. "		2 " 4 in. "	"	"	"		4.75
" 6 "	"	2 " 4 in. "	"	"	"		5.00
" 6 " 6 in. "		2 " 4 in. "	"	"	"		5.50
" 7 "	"	2 " 4 in. "	"	"	"		6.00
" 7 " 6 in. "		2 " 4 in. "	"	"	"		6.50
" 8 "	"	2 " 4 in. "	"	"	"		7.00
" 8 " 6 in. "		2 " 4 in. "	"	"	"		8.50

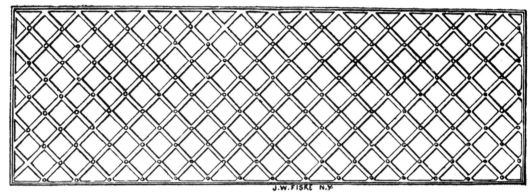

FIG. 14 K

Cast Iron Box Stall Guard.

Box Stall Guards, 2 feet 4 inches high, any length, made in one piece, to 9 feet 6 inches.

Per lineal foot.............................$1.50 | Feeding Doors in head pieces, each, net.......$4.00
"   "   " 2 feet high.................. 1.20 |

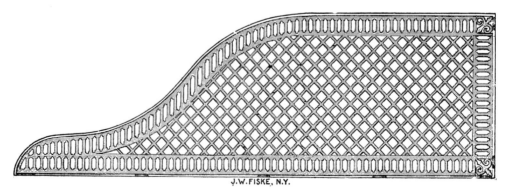

FIG. 15 K

Cast Iron Stall Guard.

Size. 7 feet	long,	2 feet 6 inches high, each			$ 9.50
" 7 " 6 in. "		2 " 6 " " "			10.00
" 8 "	"	2 " 6 " " "			10.50
" 8 " 6 in. "		2 " 6 " " "			11.00
Box Stall Guards, 2 feet 6 inches high, any length, made to order, per lineal foot..............					1.75

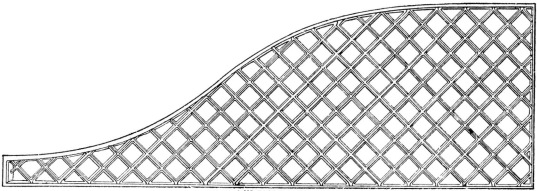

FIG. 16 K

Cast Iron Stall Guard.

Size, 7 feet long, 2 feet 10 inches high, round end, each						....	$ 8.00
" 7 " 6 in. " 2 " 10 " " square " "						....	8.50
" 8 " " 2 " 10 " " " " "						....	9.00
" 8 " 6 in. " 2 " 10 " " " " "						....	10.00
" 9 " " 2 " 10 " " " " "						....	10.50
" 9 " 6 in. " 2 " 10 " " " " "						....	11.50

FIG. 17 K

Cast Iron Box Stall Guard.

Box Stall Guards, 2 feet 10 inches high, any length, made in one piece, to 10 feet

Per lineal foot............................$1.70 | Feeding Doors in head pieces, each, net......$4.00

FIG. 18 K

Cast Iron Stall Guard.

Size, 7 feet long, 2 feet 6 inches high, each			....	$8.00
" 7 " 6 in. " 2 " 6 " " "			....	8.50
" 8 " " 2 " 6 " " "			....	9.00
" 8 " 6 in. " 2 " 6 " " "			....	9.50
Box Stall Guards, 2 feet 6 inches high, any length, made to order, per lineal foot			....	2.00

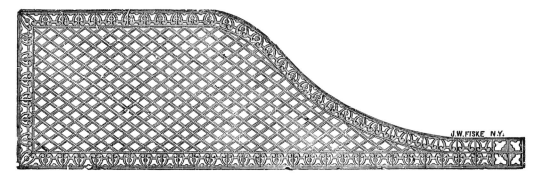

FIG. 19 K

Cast Iron Stall Guard.—(Design Patented.)

Size, 7 feet		long,	2	feet	8	inches high, square end. each					$12.00
" 7 " 6 in.	"		2	"	8	"	"	"	"	"	13.00
" 8 "		"	2	"	8	"	"	"	"	"	14.00
" 8 " 6 in.	"		2	"	8	"	"	"	"	"	15.00
" 9 "		"	2	"	8	"	"	"	"	"	16.00
" 9 " 6 in.	"		2	"	8	"	"	"	"	"	18.00
" 10 "		"	2	"	8	"	"	"	"	"	20.00

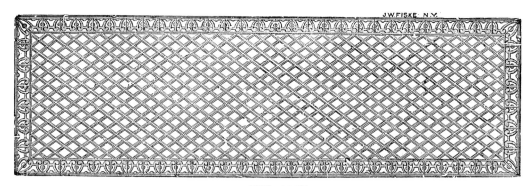

FIG. 20 K

Cast Iron Stall Guard.—(Design Patented.)

Box Stall Guards, 2 feet 8 inches high, any length, made in one piece, to 10 feet.

Per lineal foot.. $2.75
Feeding Doors in head pieces, each, net.. 4.00

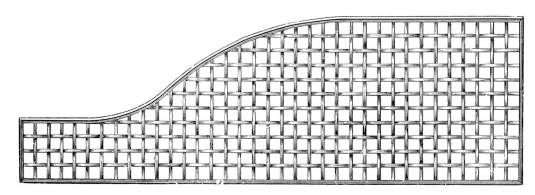

FIG. 21 K

Flat Wrought Iron Stall Guard.

Made of ⅜ inch flat iron, in wrought iron frame.

Per square foot...$0.60

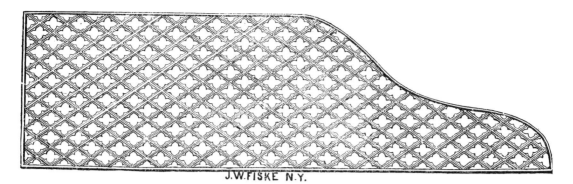

FIG. 22 K

Cast Iron Stall Guard.

Size, 6 feet	long, 2 feet 1 inch high, round end, each							....	$6.00
" 6 " 6 in.	" 2 " 1 "	"	"	"	"			....	6.50
" 7 "	" 2 " 1 "	"	"	"	"			....	7.00
" 7 " 6 in.	" 2 " 1 "	"	"	"	"			....	7.50
" 8 "	" 2 " 1 "	"	"	"	"			....	8.00

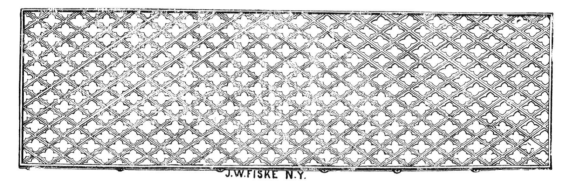

FIG. 23 K

Cast Iron Box Stall Guard.

Box Stall Guards, 2 feet 1 inch high, any length, made in one piece, to 9 feet 6 inches.

Per lineal foot..$1.60

Feeding Doors in head pieces, each, net.. 4.00

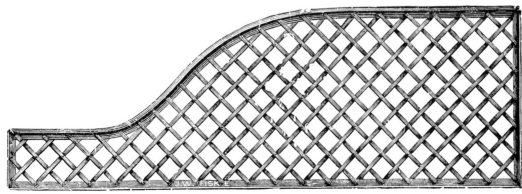

FIG. 24 K

Wrought Iron Stall Guard.

7 feet	long, 2 feet 4 inches high, each.....						....	$17.00
7 " 6 in. "	2 " 4 "	"	"				....	18.00
8 "	" 2 " 4 "	"	"				....	19.00
8 " 6 in. "	2 " 4 "	"	"				....	20.00
9 "	" 2 " 4 "	"	"				....	21.00

Box Stall Guards, 2 feet 4 inches high, any length, made to order, per lineal foot.................... 2.50

The above Guard is of flat Wrought Iron, 3 inches diamond mesh, riveted, with T Iron Frame, making a very strong guard.

Sheet Iron Panel Ends, as shown on Fig. 30 K, add $6.00 to each list.

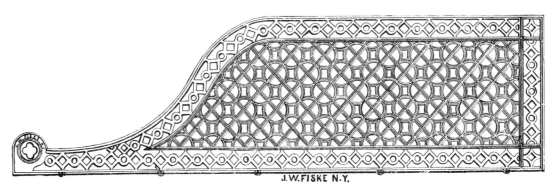

FIG. 25 K

Cast Iron Stall Guard.

Size, 8 feet   long, 2 feet 6 inches high, each.. $11.50
" 8 " 8 in. " 2 " 6 " " " 13.00
" 9 " 6 in. " 2 " 6 " " " 14.00

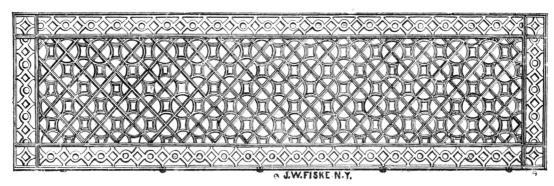

FIG. 26 K

Cast Iron Box Stall Guard.

Box Stall Guards, 2 feet 6 inches high, any length, made in one piece, to 10 feet.

Per lineal foot... $1.75
Feeding Doors in head pieces, each, net... 4.00

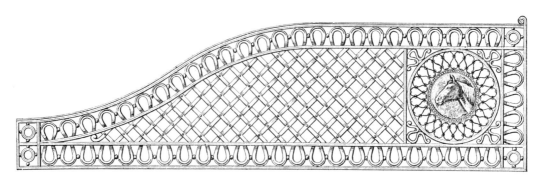

FIG. 27 K

Wrought and Cast Iron Stall Guard.

Size, 8 feet   long, 2 feet 6 inches high, each.. $30.00
" 8 " 6 in " 2 " 6 " " " 32.00
" 9 " " 2 " 6 " " " 34.00
" 9 " 6 in. " 2 " 6 " " " 36.00
Box Stall Guards, 2 feet 6 inches high, any length, made to order, per lineal foot.................. 3.50
Sheet Iron Panel Ends, as shown on Fig. 30 K, add $6.00 to each list.

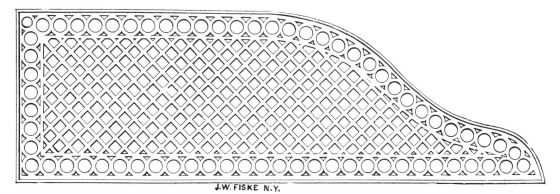

FIG. 28 K

Cast Iron Stall Guard.

Size, 5 feet		long, 2 feet 2 inches high, round end, each							$ 5.00
" 5 " 6 in.	"	2 " 2	"	"	"	"	"		5.50
" 6 "	"	2 " 2	"	"	"	"	"		6.00
" 6 " 6 in.	"	2 " 2	"	"	"	"	"		6.50
" 7 "	"	2 " 2	"	"	"	"	"		7.00
" 7 " 6 in.	"	2 " 2	"	"	"	"	"		7.50
" 8 "	"	2 " 2	"	"	square	"	"		8.50
" 8 " 6 in.	"	2 " 2	"	"	"	"	"		9.50
" 9 "	"	2 " 2	"	"	"	"	"		11.00

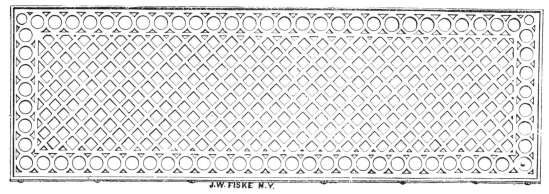

FIG. 29 K

Cast Iron Box Stall Guard.

Box Stall Guards, 2 feet 2 inches high, any length, made in one piece, to 9 feet.

Per lineal foot.............................$1.65 | Feeding Doors in head pieces, each, net......$4.00

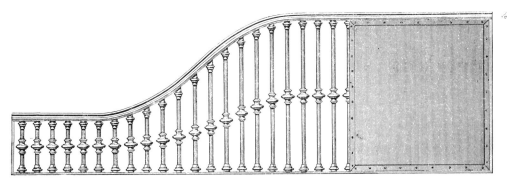

FIG. 30 K

**Wrought Iron Stall Guard, with Cast Ornaments, and Moulded Wrought Iron Cap Rail, with Sheet
Iron Panel End.**

Size, 8 feet		long, 2 feet 4 inches high, ½ inch round iron uprights, each					$19.00
" 8 6 in	"	2 " 4	"	"	½ "	"	20.50
" 9	"	2 " 4	"	"	1½ "	"	22.00
" 9 6 in.	"	2 " 4	"	"	½ "	"	23.50
Box Stall Guards, 2 feet 4 inches high, any length made to order, per lineal foot							2.60

Panel ends, extra. Add $6.00 to each list.

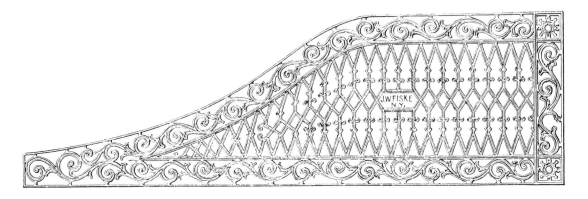

FIG. 31 K

Cast Iron Stall Guard.

Size, 7 feet 6 inches long, 2 feet 8 inches high, square end, each.................................. $11.00
    " 8 "   " 2 " 8 "   "   "   " 12.00
    " 8 " 6 "   " 2 " 8 "   "   "   " 13.00
    " 9 "   " 2 " 8 "   "   "   " 14.00
    " 9 " 6 "   " 2 " 8 "   "   "   " 15.00

FIG. 32 K

Cast Iron Box Stall Guard.

Box Stall Guards, 2 feet 8 inches high, any length, in one piece, to 9 feet 2 inches.

Per lineal foot.. $2.40
Feeding Doors in head pieces, each, net... 4.00

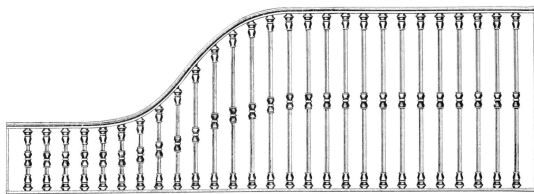

FIG. 33 K

	⅝ inch round iron uprights	¾ inch round iron uprights
Size, 8 feet long, 2 feet 4 inches high, each....................	$18.00	$20.00
" 8 " 6 in. " 2 " 4 " "	19.00	21.00
" 9 " " 2 " 4 " "	20.50	22.50
" 9 " 6 in. " 2 " 4 " "	21.50	23.50
Box Stall Guards, 2 feet 4 inches high, any length made to order, per lineal foot..................	2.00	3.00

Sheet Iron Panel Ends, as shown on Fig. 30 K. add $6.00 to each list.

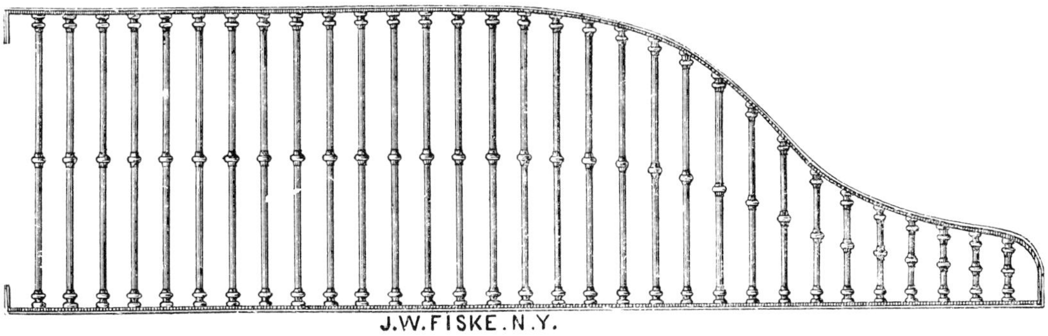
J.W.FISKE.N.Y.

FIG. 34 K

Wrought Iron Stall Guard with Cast Ornaments.

Size, 5 feet	long, 2 feet 4 inches high,	$\frac{1}{2}$ inch round uprights,	round end,	each	$ 9.50
" 6 "	" 2 " 4 " "	$\frac{1}{2}$ "	"	"	11.00
" 7 "	" 2 " 4 " "	$\frac{1}{2}$ "	"	"	12.00
" 7 " 6 in.	" 2 " 4 " "	$\frac{1}{2}$ "	"	"	13.00
" 8 "	" 2 " 4 " "	$\frac{1}{2}$ "	square end,		14.00
" 8 " 6 in.	" 2 " 4 " "	$\frac{1}{2}$ "	"	"	15.00
" 9 "	" 2 " 4 " "	$\frac{1}{2}$ "	"	"	16.00
" 9 " 6 in.	" 2 " 4 " "	$\frac{1}{2}$ "	"	"	17.50

Sheet Iron Panel Ends, as shown in Fig. 30 K, add $6.00 to each list.

This Guard made with continuous frame on end if desired.

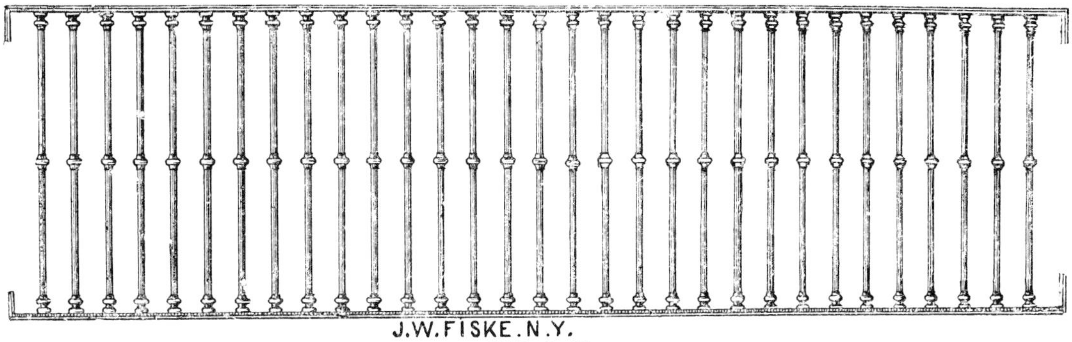
J.W.FISKE.N.Y.

FIG. 35 K

Wrought Iron Box Stall Guard, with Cast Ornaments.

Box Stall Guards, 2 feet 4 inches high, any length, per lineal foot.................................$2.10

Feeding Doors in head pieces, each, net.. 4.00

This Guard made with continuous frames on ends if desired.

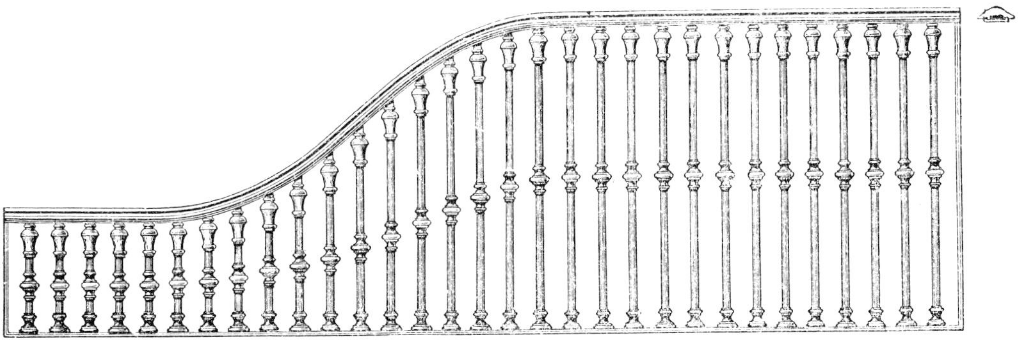

FIG. 36 K

Wrought Iron Stall Guard with Cast Ornaments.

With moulded Wrought Iron Cap Rail.

Size, 8 feet	long, 2 feet 4 inches high,	$\frac{5}{8}$ inch round iron uprights,		each	$19.00
" 8 " 6 in.	" 2 " 4 " "	$\frac{5}{8}$ "	"	"	20.50
" 9 "	" 2 " 4 " "	$\frac{5}{8}$ "	"	"	22.00
" 9 " 6 in.	" 2 " 4 " "	$\frac{5}{8}$ "	"	"	23.50

Box Stall Guards, 2 feet 4 inches high, any length, made to order, per lineal foot.................. $2.85

Sheet Iron Panel Ends, as shown on Fig. 30 K add $6.00 to each list.

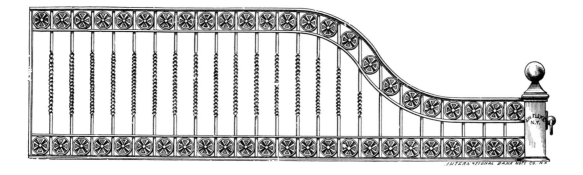

Wrought Iron Stall Guard, with Cast Ornaments.

Size, 8 feet   long, 2 feet 4 inches high, ½ inch square iron uprights, each $20.00
"   8 " 6 in.   "   2 " "   "   "   ½   "   "   " 21.00
"   9 "   "   2 "   "   "   ½   "   "   " 22.00
"   9 " 6 in.   "   2   "   "   "   ½   "   "   " 23.00
Box Stall Guards, 2 feet 4 inches high, any length, per lineal foot............................... 2.75
Post Caps, each... 4.50
       Sheet Iron Panel Ends, as shown on Fig. 43 K add $6.00 to each list.

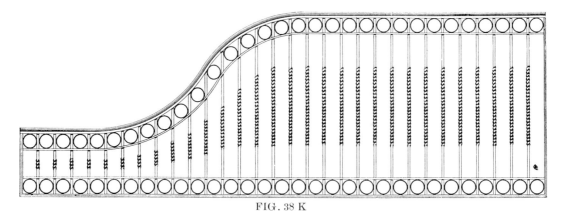

FIG. 38 K

Size, 8 feet   long, 2 feet 4 inches high, ½ inch square iron uprights, each.........................$19.00
"   8 " 6 in.   "   2 " 4   "   ½   "   "   " 20.00
"   9 "   "   2 " 4   "   ½   "   "   " 21.00
"   9 " 6 in.   "   2 " 4   "   ½   "   "   " 22.00
Box Stall Guards, 2 feet 4 inches high, any length, made to order, per lineal foot................. 2.75
       Sheet Iron Panel Ends, as shown on Fig. 43 K add $6.00 to each list.

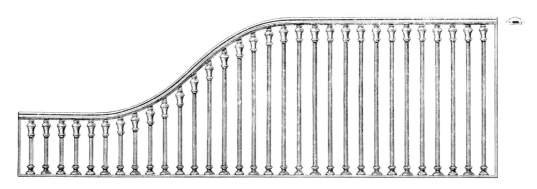

FIG 39 K

Wrought Iron Stall Guard, with Cast Iron Ornaments.

With moulded Wrought Iron Cap Rail.

	⅝ inch round iron uprights	¾ inch round iron uprights
Size, 8 feet long, 2 feet 4 inches high, each...........................	$18.00	$20.00
" 8 " 6 in. " 2 " 4 " " "	19.00	21.00
" 9 " " 2 " 4 " " "	20.50	22.50
" 9 " 6 in. " 2 " 4 " " "	21.50	23.50
Box Stall Guards, 2 feet 4 inches high, any length, made to order, per lineal foot.....	$2.00	3.00

       Sheet Iron Panel ends, as shown in Fig. 43 K add $6.00 to each list.

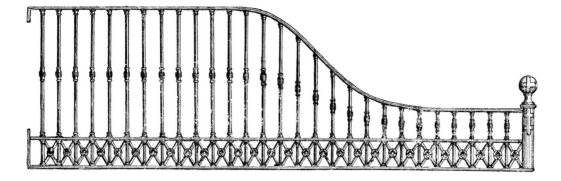

FIG. 40 K

Wrought Iron Stall Guard, with Cast Ornaments and Ornamental Post Cap.

Size, 8 feet 6 inches long, 2 feet 4 inches high, ½ inch round iron uprights, each.........................$20.00
" 9 "   "   " 2 " 4   "   ½   "   "   " 21.00
" 9 " 6   "   " 2 " 4   "   ½   "   "   " 22.00
" 10 "   "   " 2 " 4   "   ½   "   "   " 23.00
Post Caps, each.......... .... 4.50
Box Stall Guards, 2 feet 4 inches high, any length, per lineal foot......... .... 2.60
    Sheet Iron Panel Ends, as shown on Fig. 43 K add $6.00 to each list.

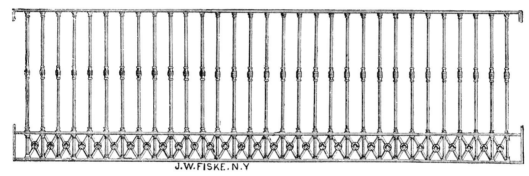

J.W.FISKE.N.Y

FIG. 41 K

Wrought Iron Box Stall Guard, with Cast Ornaments.

Box Stall Guards, 2 feet 4 inches high, any length, per lineal foot... ....$2.60
Feeding Doors in head pieces, each, net................ .... 4.00

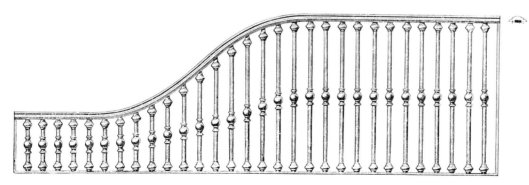

FIG. 42 K

Wrought Iron Stall Guard, with Cast Iron Ornaments.

With Moulded Wrought Iron Cap Rail.

Size, 8 feet   long 2 feet 4 inches high, ⅝ inch round iron uprights, each $19.00
" 8 " 6 in.   " 2 " 4   "   ⅝   "   "   " 20.50
" 9 "   " 2 " 4   "   ⅝   "   "   " 22.00
" 9 " 6 in.   " 2 " 4   "   ⅝   "   "   " 23.50
Box Stall Guards, 2 feet 4 inches high, any length, made to order, per lineal foot.................... 2.85
Sheet Iron Panel Ends, as shown on Fig. 43 add $6.00 to each list.

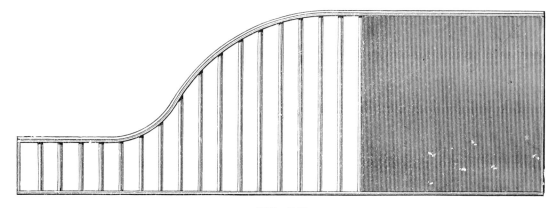

FIG. 43 K

Wrought Iron Stall Guard, with Sheet Iron Panel Ends.

		½ inch round iron uprights	⅝ inch round iron uprights
Size, 8 feet long, 2 feet 4 inches high		$13.00	$15.50
" 8 " 6 in. " 2 " 4 "		14.00	16.50
" 9 " " 2 " 4 "		14.50	17.25
" 9 " 6 in " 2 " 4 "		15.25	18.25

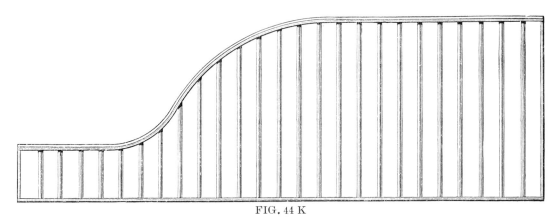

FIG. 44 K

Wrought Iron Stall Guard.

		½ inch round iron uprights	⅝ inch round iron uprights
Size, 5 feet long, 2 feet 4 inches high		$ 6.00	$ 7.50
" 6 " " 2 " 4 "		7.50	9.50
" 7 " " 2 " 4 "		9.00	11.25
" 8 " " 2 " 4 "		10.50	13.00
" 8 " 6 in. " 2 " 4 "		11.25	14.00
" 9 " " 2 " 4 "		12.00	14.75
" 9 " 6 in. " 2 " 4 "		12.75	15.75

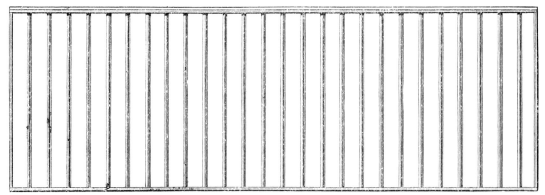

FIG. 45 K

Wrought Iron Box Stall Guard.

	½ inch round iron uprights	⅝ inch round iron uprights
Box Stall Guards, 2 feet 4 inches high, any length made to order, per lineal foot	$1.10	$1.50

Feeding Doors in head pieces, each, net $4.00.

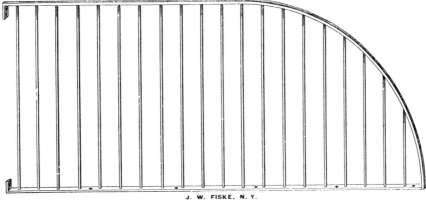

FIG. 46 K

Wrought Iron Stall Guard, with High Round End.

Size, 4 feet long, 2 feet 4 inches high, $\frac{1}{2}$ inch round iron uprights, each.........................$5.50
" 4 " 6 in. " 2 " 4 " $\frac{1}{2}$ " " " 6.50
" 5 " " 2 " 4 " $\frac{1}{2}$ " " " 7.50
" 5 " 6 in. " 2 " 4 " $\frac{1}{2}$ " " " 8.50

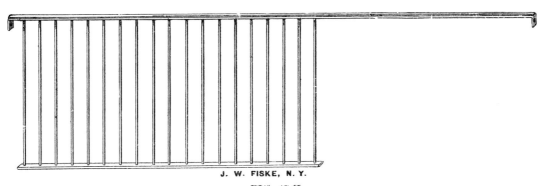

FIG. 47 K

Wrought Iron Stall Guard, with Extended Top Frame.

Size, 4 feet long, 2 feet 4 inches high, $\frac{1}{2}$ inch round iron uprights, each.........................$6.50
" 4 " 6 in. " 2 " 4 " $\frac{1}{2}$ " " " 7.50
" 5 " " 5 " 4 " $\frac{1}{2}$ " " " 8.50

The above sizes refer to Guard; price includes extended top frame.

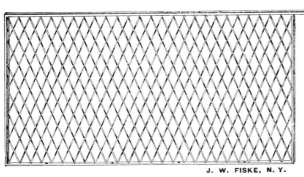

FIG. 48 K

Crimped Wire Diamond Pattern Stall Guard, with Extended Top Frame.

Per Square foot, including extended frame...$0.60
The above price refers to the Guard, but includes extended top frame.

Any size mesh and wire made to order. The above Guards are particularly adapted for stables where economy is desired, being higher in proportion to the length than ordinary O. G. Guards of same length.

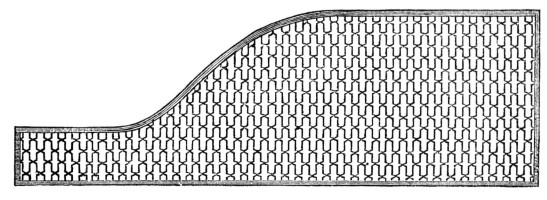

FIG. 49 K

Stall Guard.

Side Crimp Pattern Stall Guard, per square foot.............. ....$0.60

Any size mesh and wire made to order.

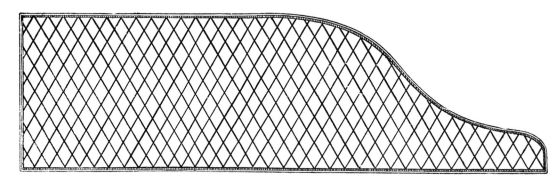

FIG. 50 K

Stall Guard.

Crimp Wire, Diamond Pattern Stall Guard, per square foot................................ ....$0.50

Any size mesh and wire made to order.

J.W.FISKE.N.Y.

FIG. 51 K

Box Stall Guard.

Box Stall Guard, per square foot. $0.50

Any size wire and mesh made to order.

Feeding Doors in head pieces, each, net................................ ....$4.00

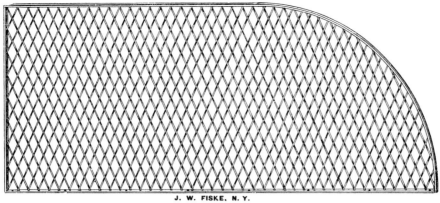

J. W. FISKE, N. Y.

FIG. 52 K

Crimped Wire Stall Guard, with High Round End.

Particularly adapted for stables where economy is desired, the round end being higher in proportion than ordinary O. G. Guards of same length.

Per square foot.......... ... .$0.50

Any size wire and mesh made to order.

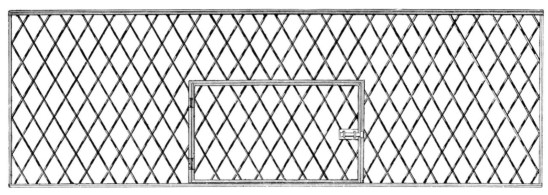

FIG. 53 K

Showing Wire Guard at Head of Stall with Feeding Door.

Can be made of any Pattern Guard, at regular price per square foot.

For making Feeding Door....... ....$6.00

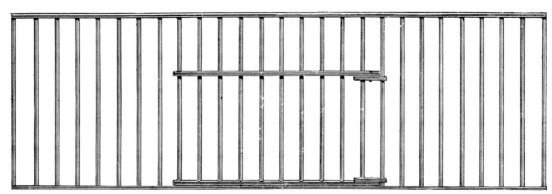

FIG. 54 K

Showing Wrought Iron Guard at Head of Stall with Feeding Door.

Can be made of any Pattern Guard, at regular price per lineal foot.

For making Feeding Door.......... ....$6.00

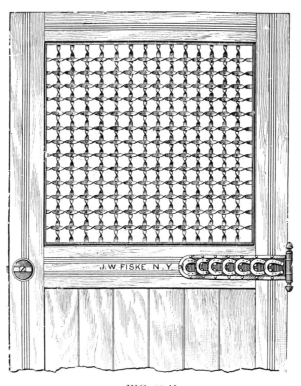

FIG. 55 K

Box Stall Door Guard.

The above illustrates the strongest and most desirable way of making Box Stall Doors, the guard being put in a panel, with screws all around.

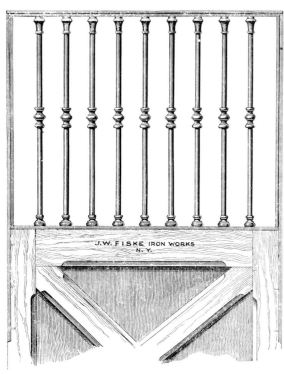

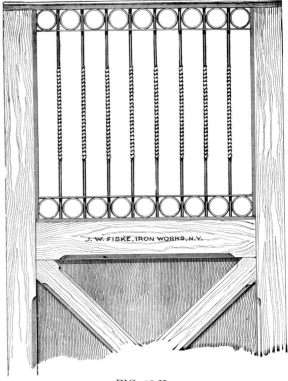

FIG. 56 K

Showing method of fastening door guard, of any pattern on top of door, with wrought iron straps on each side, which should be sunken flush with door stiles.

Add to price of Guards for wrought iron straps, for each door $2.00

FIG. 57 K

The above illustrates manner of fastening door guard at sides and bottom. The top frame extending to outer edge of door stile.

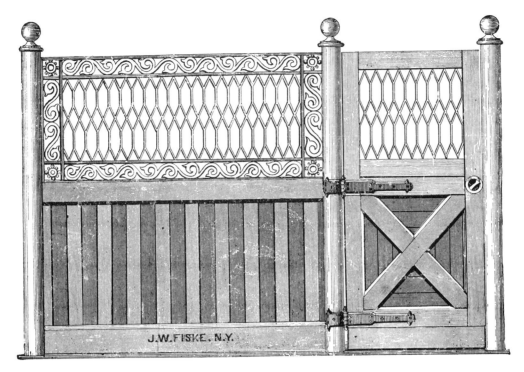

FIG. 58 K

The above shows our Box Stall fitted with Fig. 32 K Guard. Attention is called to the manner of putting in the guard for door, being the most desirable way of securing same.

FIG. 59 K

The above illustration shows a box and open stall, fitted with Fiske's Sanitary Stall Drains.   Special attention is called to the heavy and massive fittings, also the low partition in front of box stall, and door to match, which is made in a wrought iron frame. The cap and sill rails are of iron, the latter being elevated above the floor line, which prevents the decaying of the wood, forming stall partitions. See Fig. 60 K, No. 4. Prices will be given on application, when plans and specifications are furnished.

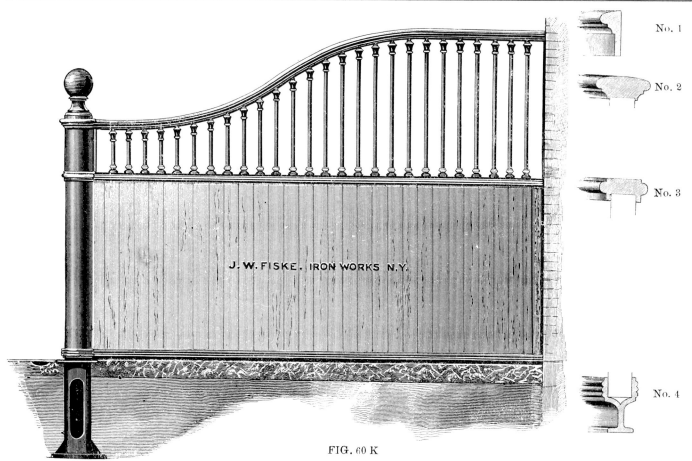

FIG. 60 K

The above illustration shows exceptionally heavy and massive fittings, samples of which may be seen at our warerooms, and prices will be given from plans and specifications. Special attention is called to above design, including the Posts. Guard, Wainscot Rail, also cap and Sill Rail, the latter being elevated above the floor line, making it impossible for the Stall Partitions to decay. The Posts are made for either wood, brick or concrete floor, and with either iron, brass or bronze post caps.

FIG. 61 K

The above illustration shows a box and open stall, fitted with Fiske's Sanitary Stall Drains, and the fittings are of the same general style as Fig. 59 K and 60 K. Special attention is called to the framing of the box stall door, posts and sill rail. Special prices given on application from plans and specifications.

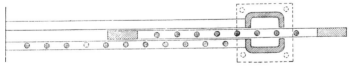

FIG. 62 K

Showing Box Stalls with sliding doors and sectional plan, showing method of sliding door into partition.

Fig. 323 K Post is herewith illustrated, which admits the door to slide through post and between double front partitions. Doors are fastened by flush bolt at the back of post, making it impossible for the horse to open the door. The track on which the door hangers are hung, is concealed by iron moulding. This mode of arranging doors is especially recommended where it is impossible to hang a door on hinges.

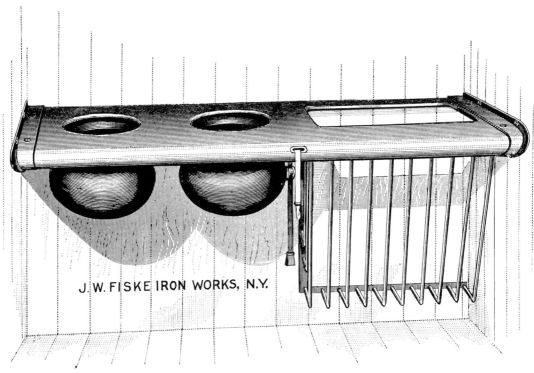

FIG. 63 K

Wrought Iron Hay Rack, Cast Oat Manger and Water Pot.—One Fixture.—Very Heavy.

This Fixture can, by extension attachments at either end be made to fit any stall from 5 feet 5 inches to 6 feet 4 inches in width. Water pot can be provided with brass plug, strainer and coupling for drawing off the water.

	Painted	Water Pot and Manger Galvanized	Water Pot and Manger Enamelled
Size, 5 feet 5 inches long, 24 inches wide, each....	$42.00	$47.00	$50.00
" 6 " 4 " " "	47.00	52.00	55.00

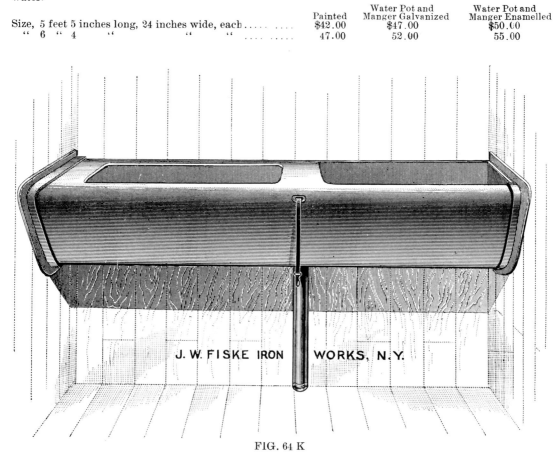

FIG. 64 K

Hay Rack and Manger.—One Fixture.

This Fixture is a copy of those made in England and in use in many stables of the nobility of Europe. Is a very massive Fixture and specially designed for private stables, where elegance and durability is a feature. Can be made to fit any stall from 4 feet 10 inches to 5 feet 3 inches in width.

Size, 4 feet 10 inches to 5 feet 3 inches long, 20 inches wide. Prices given on application.

FIG. 65 K

Hay Rack and Manger.—One Fixture.

Especially adapted for private stables where something massive and elegant is required. So arranged that it is impossible for the horse to be injured in any way.

Made with movable fixtures arranged to accommodate stalls from 4 ft. 9 in. to 5 ft. in width.

Size, 4 feet 9 inches to 5 feet long, 24 inches wide, each....................................$40.00

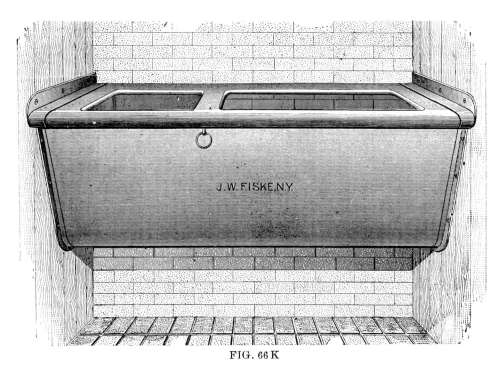

FIG. 66 K

Hay Rack and Manger.—One Fixture.

Especially adapted for private stables, being massive and substantial. On account of the smooth surface and sloping front, offers practically no possible opportunity for injury to the horse. Made with movable fixtures, arranged to accommodate stalls from 4 feet 9 inches to 5 feet in width.

Size, 4 feet 9 inches to 5 feet long, 24 inches wide, each....................................$37.00

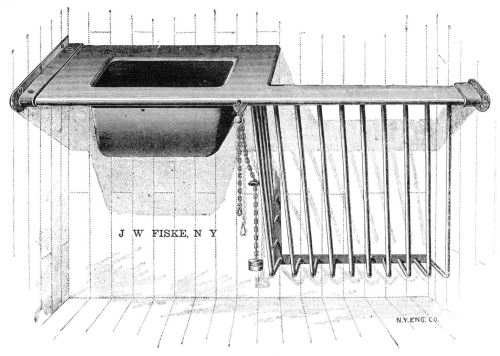

FIG. 67 K

Wrought Iron Hay Rack and Cast Oat Manger.—One Fixture.

Made right and left.

With Food Guard all around, which effectually prevents the horse throwing out his oats. The Halter Chain, which passes over a pulley, with variable weight and India Rubber Buffer, are all valuable improvements.

	Painted	Manger Galvanized	Manger Enameled
Each....	$24.00	$27.00	$29.00

This fixture can, by extension attachments at either end, be made to fit any stall from 4 feet to 5 feet in width.

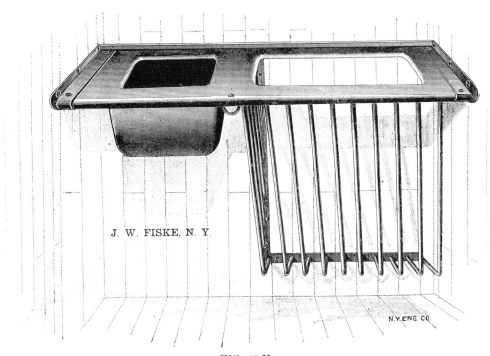

FIG. 68 K

Wrought Iron Hay Rack and Cast Oat Manger.—One Fixture.

With food guard all around, which effectually prevents the horse throwing out his oats.

	Painted	Manger Galvanized	Manger Enameled
Size, 4 feet 6 inches long, 21 inches wide, each......................	$19.00	$21.50	$24.00
" 4 " 6 " to 5 feet long, 21 inches wide, each..............	21.00	23.50	26.00

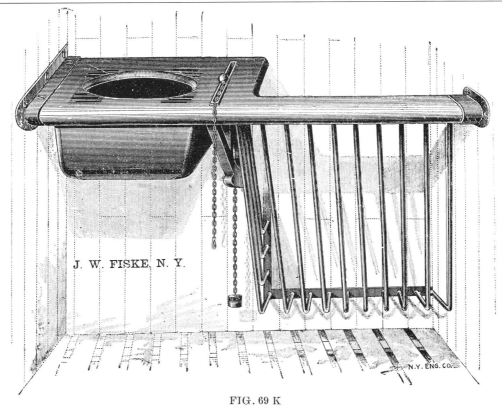

FIG. 69 K

Wrought Iron Hay Rack and Cast Oat Manger.—One Fixture.

Made right and left.

With Food Guard all around, which effectually prevents the horse throwing out his oats. The Halter Chain, which passes over a pulley within a hollow bracket with variable weight and India Rubber Buffer, are all valuable improvements.

This fixture can, by extension attachments at either end, be made to fit any stall from 4 feet to 5 feet in width.

	Painted	Manger Galvanized	Manger Enameled
Size, 4 feet 6 inches to 4 feet 8 inches, each..............	$26.00	$29.00	$31.00
" 4 " 8 " 4 " 10 " "	27.00	30.00	32.00
" 4 " 10 " 5 " each........................	28.00	31.00	33.00

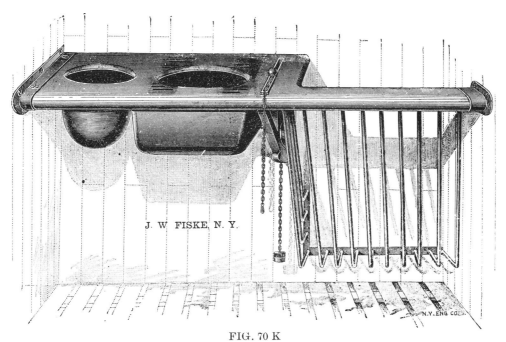

FIG. 70 K

Wrought Iron Hay Rack, Cast Oat Manger and Water Pot.—One Fixture.

	Painted	Water Pot and Manger Galvanized	Water Pot and Manger Enameled
This fixture can, by extension attachments at either end, be made to fit any stall from 5 feet 4 inches to 5 feet 8 inches in width, each...............................	$40.00	$46.00	$50.00

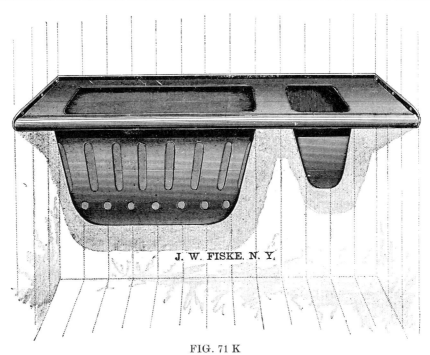

FIG. 71 K

Hay Box and Oat Manger.—One Fixture.—Very Heavy.

With movable ends regulating the length of fixture.

	Painted	Manger Galvanized	Manger Enameled
Size, 4 feet 6 inches long, 23 inches wide, each.....	$15.00	$18.00	$20.00
" 4 " 9 " to 5 ft. " " " "	17.50	20.50	22.50

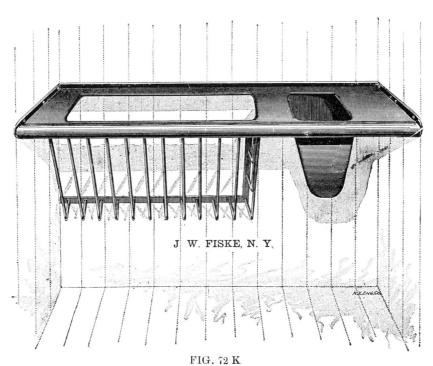

FIG. 72 K

Wrought Iron Hay Rack and Cast Oat Manger.—One Fixture.

With movable ends regulating length of fixture.

	Painted	Manger Galvanized	Manger Enameled
Size, 4 feet 6 inches long, 23 inches wide, each..........	$21.50	$25.00	$26.50
" 4 " 6 " to 5 feet long, 23 inches wide, each.............	23.50	27.00	28.50

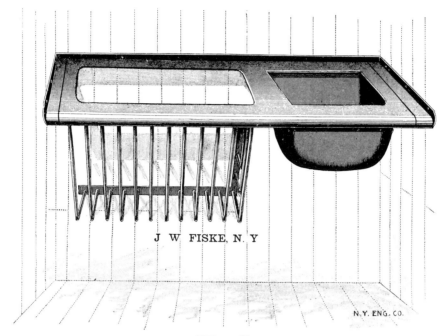

FIG. 73 K

Wrought Iron Hay Rack and Cast Oat Manger.—One Fixture.

This fixture can, by extension attachments at either end, be made to fit any stall from 4 feet 4 inches to 5 feet.   20¼ inches wide.

	Painted	Manger Galvanized	Manger Enameled
Each...	$24.00	$27.00	$29.00

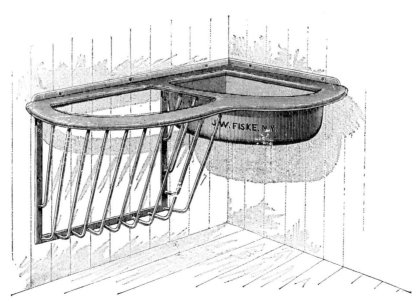

FIG. 74 K

Wrought Iron Hay Rack and Cast Oat Manger for Box Stall.—One Fixture.

	Painted	Manger Galvanized	Manger Enameled
Size, 3 feet 6 inches long, 2 feet 6 inches wide, each..............	$23.00	$27.00	$29.00

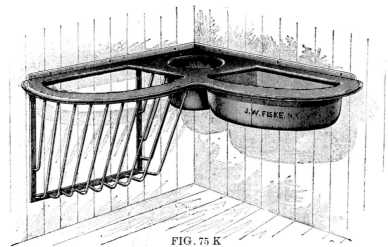

FIG. 75 K

Manger and Water Pot for Box Stall, with Wrought Iron Hay Rack.—One Fixture.

	Painted	Water Pot and Manger Galvanized	Water Pot and Manger Enamled
Size, 3 feet 5 inches long, 3 feet 5 inches wide, each..	$26.00	$32.00	$34.00

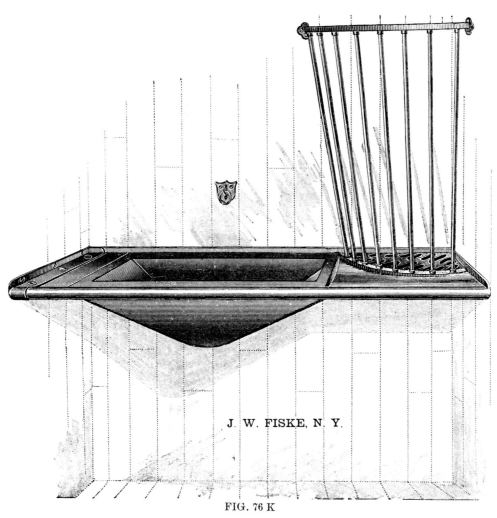

J. W. FISKE, N. Y.

FIG. 76 K

Wrought Iron Hay Rack and Cast Oat Manger.—One Fixture.

	Painted
Size, 4 feet 6 inches long, 23 inches wide, each........	$24.00
" 4 " 10 " 23 " "	27.00

This fixture can, by extension attachments at either end, be made to fit any size stall from 4 feet 6 inches to 4 feet 10 inches in width.

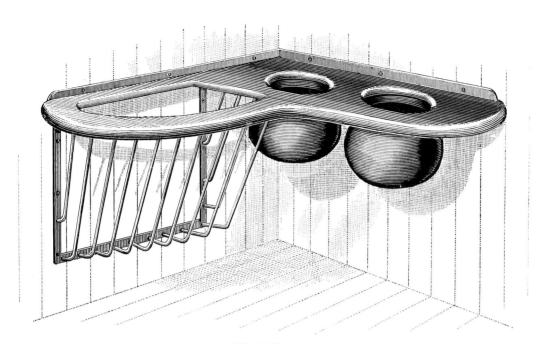

FIG. 77 K

Manger and Water Pot for Box Stall, with Wrought Iron Hay Rack.—One Fixture.—Very Heavy.

This fixture is generally used in box stalls when Fig. 63 K fixtures are used in single stalls.

	Painted	Water Pot and Manger Galvanized	Water Pot and Manger Enameled
Size, 4 feet 3 inches long, 3 feet 6 inches wide..........	$36.00	$42.00	$46.00

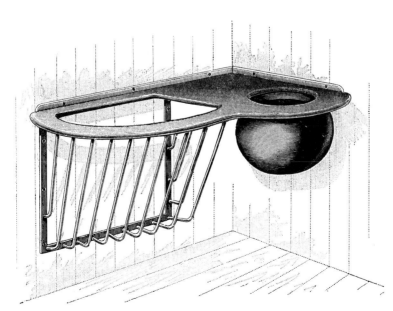

FIG. 78 K

Wrought Iron Hay Rack and Cast Oat Manger for Box Stall.—One Fixture.

	Painted	Manger Galvanized	Manger Enameled
Size, 3 feet 6 inches long, 2 feet 6 inches wide, each..........	$25.00	$28.00	$30.00

The above mangers are arranged so as to prevent horses from throwing out their oats.

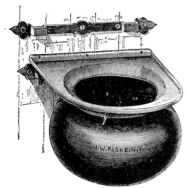

FIG. 79 K   FIG. 80 K

Detachable Back Flange Mangers for Box Stalls.

Arranged expressly to prevent horses from throwing out their oats.

	Painted	Galvanized	Enameled
Size Fig. 79 K, Length on back, 15 inches; depth, 8¾ inches; bowl, 12 inches diameter, each..........	$3.75	$6.50	$8.25
" Fig. 80 K, " " 16 " " 10½ " " 16 " "	4.75	8.00	9.75

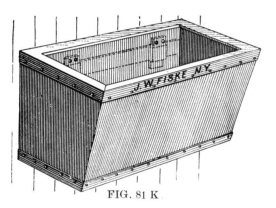

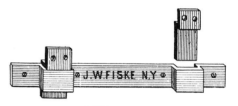

FIG. 82 K

Wrought Iron Attachment

for

FIG. 81 K   FIG. 81 K

Galvanized Iron Track Manger with Detachable Fixtures.

This manger is made of Sheet Iron, with Wrought Iron food guard all around, preventing the horse from throwing out his oats; is light and cannot get broken in transportation from one track to another; is also made with hooks to hang on if desired.

18 inches long, 11 inches deep, 11½ inches wide, each.........................$5.00

Special prices for a quantity.

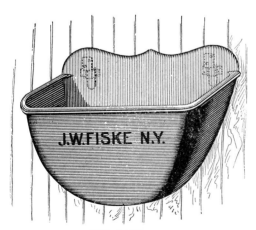

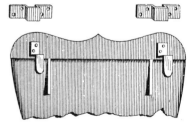

FIG. 84 K

Showing Back View of Fig. 83 K.

Back Flange Manger.

FIG. 83 K

Back Flange Manger.

Made detachable.

The above Illustrates the manner in which Fig. 83 K Manger is attached to wall.

Size, 19 inches long, 13 inches wide, each.....................................	Painted	Galvanized	Ennmeled
	$3.50	$6.00	$7.50

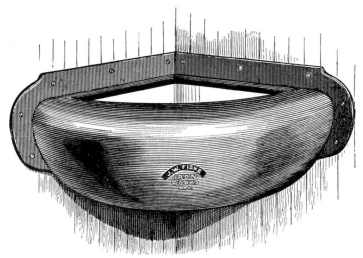

FIG. 85 K

Corner Manger.

This manger is, as may be seen by the illustration, very heavy and massive. Is a copy of the celebrated English manger, is specially designed for box stalls, when used in stables where Combination Fixtures, Fig 64 K are placed, and is of the same general character, although they can be used in single stalls, when desired.

Length on sides, 27 inches.   Depth, including flange, 15 inches.
Can be galvanized or enameled to order.   Prices given on application.

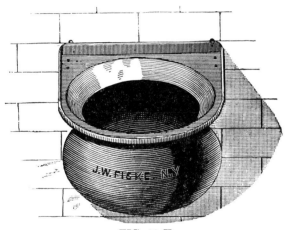

FIG. 86 K

Detachable Back Flange Manger for Box Stall.

Arranged expressly to prevent horses from throwing out their oats.

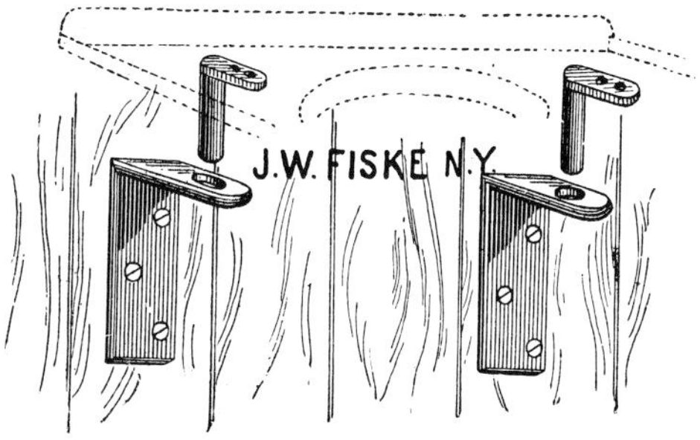

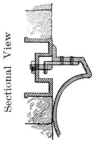

FIG. 87 K

Showing method of attaching

Fig. 86 K Manger to wood.

Length on back, 16 inches; depth 10½ inches; bowl, 15 inches diameter.

Plain, each...........painted, $4.75   Galvanized............$8.00   Enameled... ... .$9.75

FIG. 88 K

FIG. 89 K

Showing the method of attaching Fig. 86 K Manger to brick wall, leaving no projection when Manger is removed.
Casting one piece, each.. .... $1.50

FIG. 90 K

Square Manger with Feed Guard.

	Painted	Galv.	Enam.
20 in. long, 14 in. wide, 9 in. deep, each ..	$2.50	$5.50	$6.50

FIG. 91 K

Square Manger Without Food Guard.

						Painted	Galv.	Enam
18 in. long, 12 in. wide, 6 in. deep, each..						$1.50	$ 2.75	$ 4.50
19 "	13½ "	12 "	"	..		3.25	6.00	8.00
20 "	14 "	12 "	"	..		3.50	6.50	8.50
20 "	17 "	11 "	"	..		3.50	8.00	9.00
27 "	20 "	14 "	"	..		6.00	13.00	14.00

FIG. 92 K

Manger.

Principally used in Farm and Brewery Stables.

Size, 3 feet 2 inches long, 1 foot 10 inches wide, 10 inches deep, each........ ....$11.00

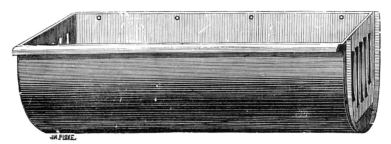

FIG. 93 K

Manger for Cut Feed.

These are so constructed that, when desired, they can be screwed together, making one continuous line of mangers the whole length of a range of stalls; can be made with solid ends when required.

Size, 4 feet 1 inch long, each................... ....$9.50

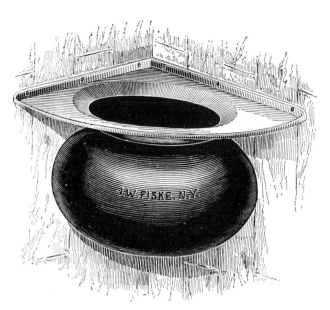

FIG. 94 K

Round Corner Manger.

TWO SIZES.

Arranged expressly to prevent horses from throwing out their oats.

No. 1. Length on sides, 17 inches; depth, 10 inches; diameter of bowl, 15 inches.

	Plain.	Galvanized.	Enameled.
Each......................	$3.75	$6.75	$9.00

No. 2. Length on sides, 16 inches; depth, 8¾ inches; diameter of bowl, 12 inches.

	Plain.	Galvanized.	Enameled.
Each............	$3.00	$6.00	$8.00

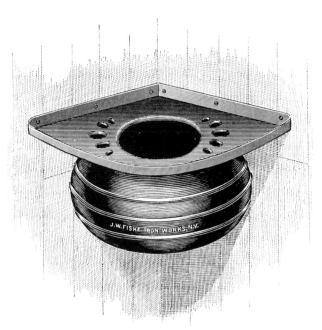

FIG. 95 K

Ventilating Corner Manger.

Made with oval opening and large food guard all around, which prevents horses from throwing out their oats.

Length on sides, 19 inches; depth, 12 inches; diameter of bowl, 18 inches.

	Plain.	Galvanized.	Enameled.
Each................. ...	$6.00	$10.00	$11.50

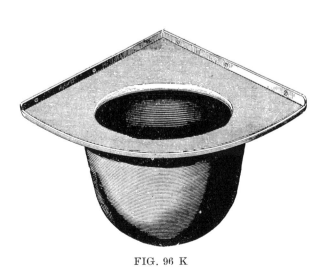

FIG. 96 K

Corner Manger.

With large food guard all around, which prevents horses from throwing out their oats.

Length on sides, 17½ inches; depth, 9½ inches; diameter of bowl, 13 inches.

	Plain.	Galvanized.	Enameled.
Each......................	$3.50	$6.50	$8.00

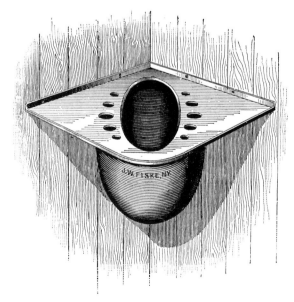

FIG. 97 K

Ventilating Corner Manger.

Made with oval opening and large food guard all around, which prevents horses from throwing out their oats.

Length on sides, 15 inches; depth, 8 inches; diameter of bowl, 12½ inches.

	Plain.	Galvanized.	Enameled.
Each......................	$3.50	$6.50	$8.00

FIG. 98 K

Corner Manger.

Length on sides, 16½ inches; depth, 9½ inches.

	Plain.	Galvanized.	Enameled.
Each............	$2.00	$4.00	$5.00

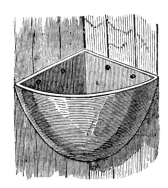

FIG. 99 K

Corner Manger.

Small size for Ponies—Length on sides, 15½ inches; depth, 8½ inches.

	Plain.	Galvanized.	Enameled.
Each....................	$1.75	$3.75	$4.75

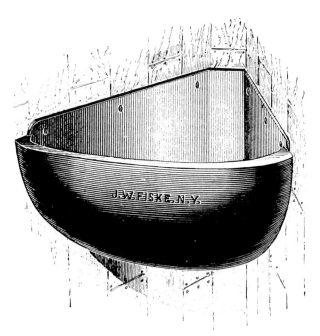

FIG. 100 K

Corner Manger.

Made on an angle to fit stalls, and is particularly adapted for narrow buildings, where it is necessary to arrange stall on an angle, in order to obtain sufficient space behind horses. One size only. Angle sent on application.

Length on sides, 16 inches; depth, 9½ inches.

	Plain.	Galvanized.	Enameled.
Each	$2.50	$5.00	$6.00

FIG. 101 K

Slow Feed Manger.

Length on sides, 17 inches; depth, 6 inches.

The cells hold 1 pint each, and prevent the horse from throwing out his oats, and a greedy animal from eating too fast.

	Plain.	Galvanized.	Enameled.
Each....................	$3.00	$4.50	$7.00

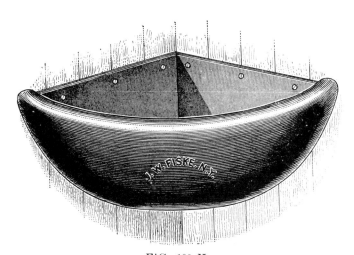

FIG. 102 K

Corner Manger.

With extra large Rolling Food Guard all around.

Length on sides, 17 inches; depth, 10 inches.

	Plain.	Galvanized.	Enameled.
Each........................	$3.50	$6.00	$7.50

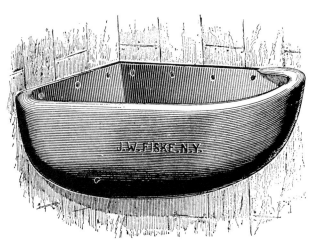

FIG. 103 K

Corner Manger, designed for Cut Feed.

Two sizes made, right and left.

No. 1. 22 inches long, 16½ inches wide; depth, 10 inches.

	Plain.	Galvanized.	Enameled.
Each....................	$4.50	$8.25	$9.50

No. 2. 25 inches long, 18 inches wide; depth, 11 inches.

	Plain.	Galvanized.	Enameled.
Each........	$5.50	$9.25	$11.00

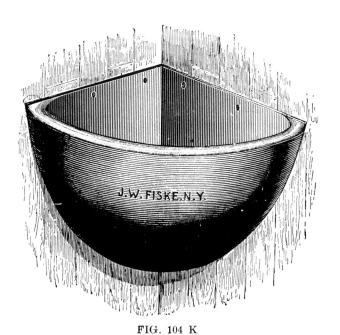

FIG. 104 K

Corner Manger.—Very Heavy.

With Rolling Food Guard all around.

Length on sides, 20 inches; depth, 12 inches.

	Plain.	Galvanized.	Enameled.
Each....................	$4.00	$6.50	$8.50

FIG. 105 K

Corner Dumping Manger.

With Food Guard on Front and Corners.

Length on sides, 17 inches; depth, 10 inches.

	Plain.	Galvanized.	Enameled.
Each....................	$3.75	$6.25	$8.00

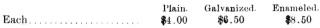

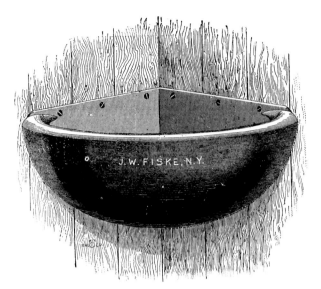

FIG. 106 K

Corner Manger.

With heavy Rolling Food Guard all around.

Length on sides, 17 inches; depth, 10 inches.

	Plain.	Galvanized.	Enameled.
Each....................	$3.50	$6.00	$8.00

FIG. 107 K

Corner Manger.

With Rolling Food Guard all around.

Length on sides, 16½ inches; depth, 9½ inches.

	Plain.	Galvanized.	Enameled.
Each....................	$3.00	$5.50	$7.00

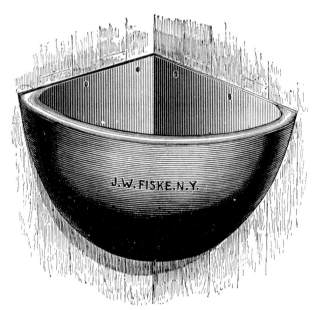

FIG. 108 K

Corner Manger.

Extra Heavy.

With heavy Rolling Food Guard all around.

Length on sides, 18 inches; depth, 12 inches.

	Plain.	Galvanized.	Enameled.
Each....................	$3.75	$6.25	$8.50

FIG. 109 K

Corner Manger.

Extra Heavy.

With Food Guard in Corners.

Length on sides, 18 inches; depth, 12 inches.

	Plain.	Galvanized.	Enameled.
Each....................	$3.00	$6.00	$8.00

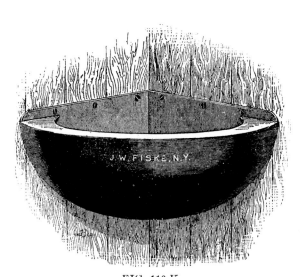

FIG. 110 K

Corner Manger.

With Food Guard all around, with Large Guard in Corners.
Length on sides, 17 inches; depth, 9½ inches.

	Plain.	Galvanized.	Enameled.
Each..................	$2.50	$5.00	$6.50

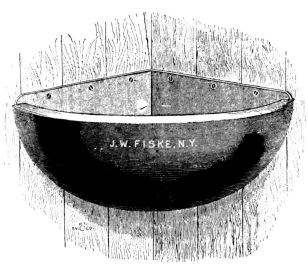

FIG. 111 K

Corner Manger.

Heavy.

With Food Guard all around.

Length on Sides, 17½ inches; depth, 10½ inches.

	Plain.	Galvanized.	Enameled.
Each..................	$2.75	$5.25	$6.50

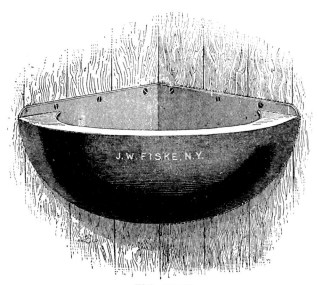

FIG. 112 K

Corner Manger.

With Food Guard all around, with Large Guard in Corners.
Length on sides, 17½ inches; depth, 10 inches.

	Plain.	Galvanized.	Enameled.
Each..................	$3.25	$5.50	$7.00

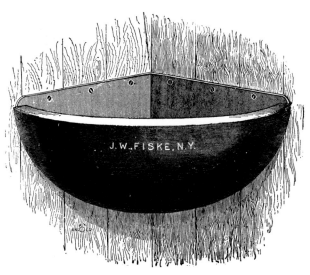

FIG. 113 K

Corner Manger.

With Food Guard all around.

Length on sides, 16 inches; depth
9½ inches, each.............. $2.25

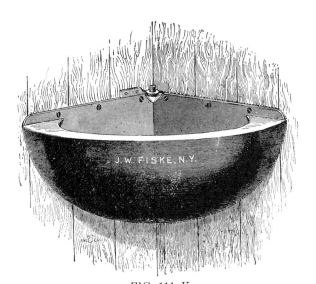

FIG. 114 K

Swinging Corner Manger.

With Food Guard all around, extra Large Guard in Corners.

Length on sides, 17½ inches; depth, 9½ inches.

	Plain.	Galvanized.	Enameled.
Each.	$4.50	$7.25	$8.50

FIG. 115 K

Swinging Corner Manger.

With Food Guard in Corners.

Length on sides, 18 inches; depth, 10 inches.

	Plain.	Galvanized.	Enameled.
Each.	$5.00	$9.00	$9.50

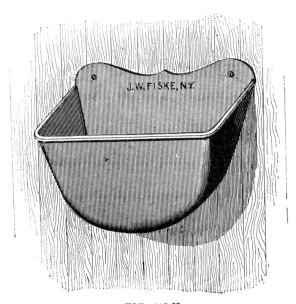

FIG. 116 K

Back Flange Manger.

Size, 19 inches long, 13 inches wide, depth, 8 inches.

	Plain.	Galvanized.	Enameled.
Each.	$3.00	$5.50	$6.50

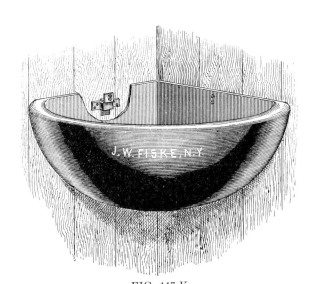

FIG. 117 K

Detachable Corner Manger.

With heavy Rolling Food Guard in front.

Length on sides, 17 inches, depth, 10 inches.

	Plain.	Galvanized.	Enameled.
Each.	$3.80	$6.30	$8.00

FIG. 2045 AK.
Rustless Steel Troughs.
Simple, Strong and Durable.
Made with cast plug in the top and bottom of one end as shown in cut for cleaning purposes.

		Painted.	Galvanized
No. 1.— 3 ft. long, 14 inches wide, 8 inches deep; made of No. 12 material.	Each.........................	$ 6.30	$ 9.45
No. 2.— 4 ft. long, 14 inches wide, 8 inches deep; made of No. 12 material.	Each.........................	6.30	9.45
No. 3.— 5 ft. long, 14 inches wide, 8 inches deep; made of No. 12 material.	Each.........................	7.85	11.80
No. 4.— 6 ft. long, 14 inches wide, 8 inches deep; made of No. 12 material.	Each.........................	9.60	14.40
No. 5.— 8 ft. long, 14 inches wide, 8 inches deep; made of No. 12 material.	Each.........................	11.70	17.55
No. 6.—10 ft. long, 14 inches wide, 8 inches deep; made of No. 12 material.	Each.........................	14.50	21.75
No. 7.— 3 ft. long, 16 inches wide, 8 inches deep; made of No. 12 material.	Each.........................	7.80	11.70
No. 8.— 4 ft. long, 16 inches wide, 9 inches deep; made of No. 12 material.	Each.........................	7.80	11.70
No. 9.— 5 ft. long, 16 inches wide, 9 inches deep; made of No. 12 material.	Each.........................	9.00	13.50
No. 10.— 6 ft. long, 16 inches wide, 9 inches deep; made of No. 12 material.	Each.........................	11.00	16.50
No. 11.— 8 ft. long, 16 inches wide, 9 inches deep; made of No. 12 material.	Each.........................	14.00	21.00
No. 12.—10 ft. long, 16 inches wide, 9 inches deep; made of No. 12 material.	Each.........................	16.65	25.00

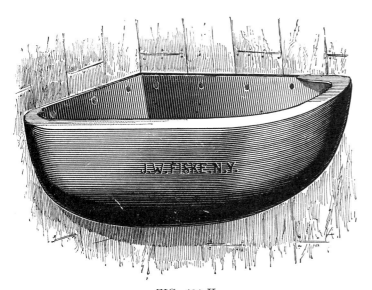

FIG. 120 K

Corner Manger.

Two Sizes.

No. 1—25 inches long, 18 inches wide; depth, 11 inches

	Plain.	Galvanized.	Enameled.
Each.............................	$5.50	$9.25	$11.00

No. 2—23 inches long, 16½ inches wide; depth, 10 inches.

	Plain.	Galvanized.	Enameled.
Each.......	$4.50	$8.25	$9.50

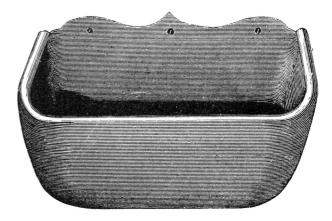

FIG. 121 K

Back Flange Manger.

24 inches long, 14 inches wide: depth, 10 inches.

	Plain.	Galvanized.	Enameled.
Each...................	$4.75	$8.25	$9.00

Made detachable.

	Plain.	Galvanized.	Enameled.
Each...................	$5.25	$8.50	$9.50

FIG. 122 K

Self-Feeding Manger.

Which absolutely prevents the horse from throwing out his oats, and also aids digestion by
limiting the supply.

22 inches long, 14 inches wide: depth, 9 inches.

	Plain.	Galvanized.	Enameled.
Each...	$5.00	$9.00	$10.00

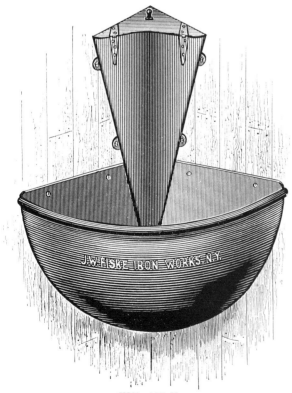

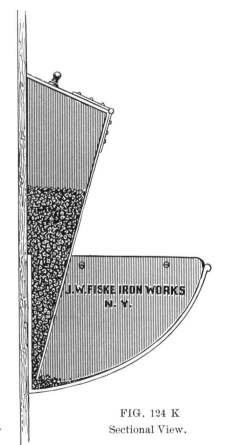

FIG. 123 K

Manger with Oat Chute.

Which absolutely prevents the horse from throwing out his oats, and also aids digestion by
limiting the supply.

FIG. 124 K

Sectional View.

Length on sides, 16½ inches; depth, 9½ inches... $3.75
Chute only, which can be applied to any corner Manger, each... 2.00

FIG. 125 K

Wall Water Trough with Back.

25 inches long, 15 inches wide, 10 inches deep.

	Painted.	Galvanized.	Enameled.
With Back, each........................	$10.00	$17.00	$22.00
Without Back, each......	7.00	10.00	14.00

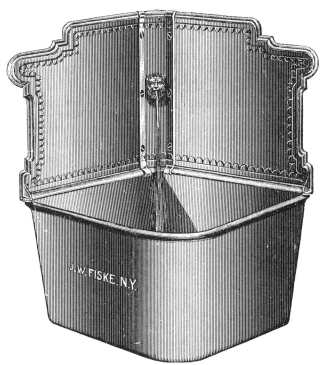

FIG. 126 K

Corner Water Trough. (Very Heavy.)

Length on sides, 18 inches; front, 21 inches; depth, 12 inches.

	Painted.	Galvanized.	Enameled.
With Back, supply pipe connection, each..	$11.00	$18.00	$23.00
Without Back, supply pipe connection, each...	7.00	$10.00	14.50

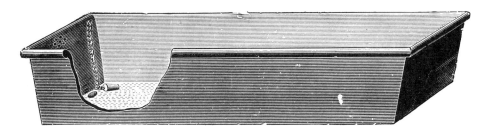

FIG. 127 K

Water Trough.

With overflow and discharge plug.

					Painted.	Galvanized.
3 feet long, 14½ inches wide, 10 inches deep, each					$10.00	$16.00
4 " 14½ " 10 " "					13.00	20.00
5 " 14½ " 10 " "					17.00	25.00
6 " 14½ " 10 " "					19.00	28.00
7 " 14½ " 10 " "					21.00	32.00
8 " 14½ " 10 " "					25.00	40.00

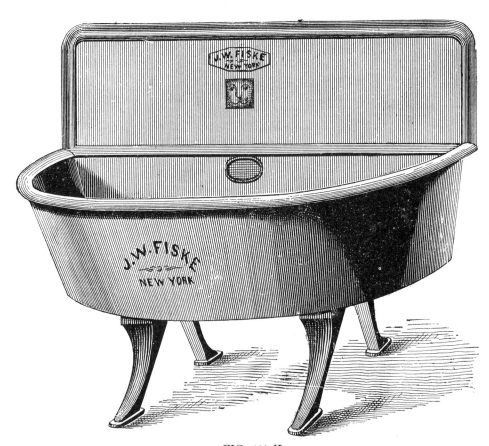

FIG. 128 K

Half Circle Water Trough.

With back and legs.

	Painted.	Galvanized.	Enameled.
3 feet 6 inches long, 18 inches wide, 10 inches deep, each	$24.00	$36.00	$38.00

Faucet can be substituted for lion's head if desired.   Extra, $1.75.

FIG. 129 K

Water Trough.

With overflow and discharge plug.

	Painted.	Galvanized.	Enameled
2 feet long, 20 inches wide, 12 inches deep, each	$ 7.00	$12.00	$14.00
3 " 20 " 12 " "	14.50	23.00	25.00
3 " 24 " 16 " "	16.00	29.00	31.00
4 " 20 " 12 " "	17.25	32.00	35.00
4 " 24 " 16 " "	22.00	38.00	40.00
5 " 20 " 12 " "	23.00	40.00	42.00
6 " 20 " 12 " "	26.00	47.00	49.00

Legs furnished when required, to above prices add $1.50 Each, net

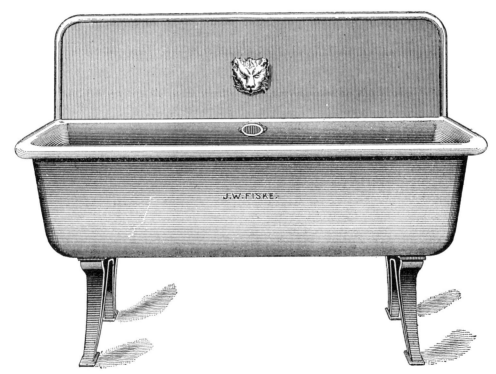

FIG. 130 K

Water Trough, with Back and Legs. Extra Heavy.

	Painted.	Galvanized.	Enameled
2 feet 6 in. long, 22 in. wide, 13 in. deep, with overflow and discharge plug	$18.00	$30.00	$32.00
3 " " 22 " 13 " " " "	20.50	33.00	35.00
3 " 6 " 22 " 13 " " " "	22.50	36.00	38.00
4 " " 22 " 13 " " " "	24.50	39.00	44.00
4 " " 22 " 18 " " " "	32.00	58.00	64.00
4 " 6 " 22 " 13 " " " "	30.00	50.00	56.00
5 " " 22 " 13 " " " "	34.00	54.00	60.00
5 " 6 " 22 " 13 " " " "	36.00	58.00	65.00
6 " " 22 " 13 " " " "	39.00	62.00	70.00

Faucet or hose connection can be substituted for lion's head if desired, at additional expense of $1.75.

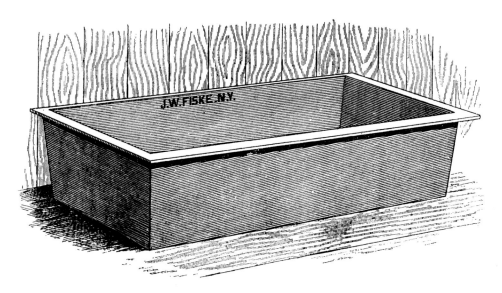

FIG. 131 K

Mixing Trough For Cut Feed.

	Painted.	Galvanized.	Enameled.
Size, 3 feet long, 20 inches wide, 12 inches deep, each....................	$16.00	$24.50	$26.50
" 3 " 24 " 16 " "	18.00	31.00	33.00
" 4 " 24 " 16 " "	25.00	41.00	43.00

FIG. 132 K

Wall Recess with Cesspool and Grating. Two Sizes.

No. 1.   29 inches high, 18½ inches wide, recess 6 inches, arranged for one or two faucets, each. $18.00
No. 2.   30 inches high, 20 inches wide, recess 8 inches, arranged for one or two faucets, each....... 19.00
Faucet, plain or with hose connection, each................... .... 1.75

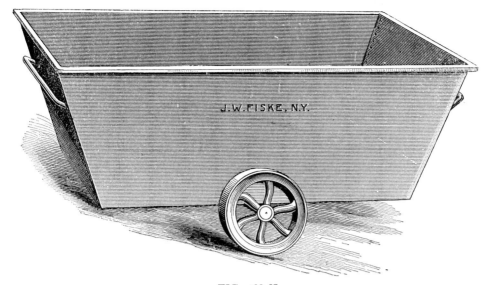

FIG. 133 K

Galvanized Sheet Iron Movable Feed Car.

Size, 48 inches long, 27 inches wide, 20 inches deep, each.................................. $50.00

Any size made to order.

FIG. 134 K

Harness Washing Sink.

Designed especially for washing harness.

The sink is so arranged that the harness can be washed without splashing the water on the floor or side wall, being of the proper height for cleaner to work conveniently.

41 inches long, 27 inches wide, 41 inches high, including legs and back.......................... $21.00
Without back... 19.00
Faucets, extra, each.. 1.75

Can be galvanized or enameled, if desired, at an additional price.

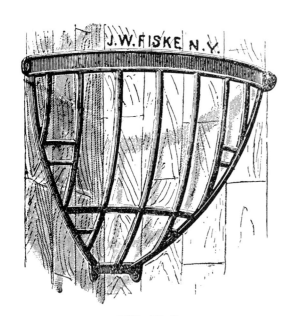

FIG. 135 K

Cast Iron Corner Hay Rack.

Each.. $2.75

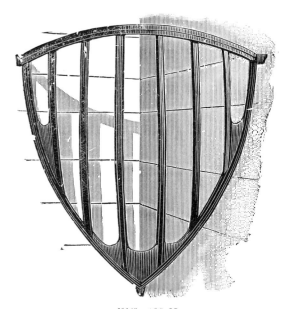

FIG. 136 K

Cast Iron Corner Hay Rack.

Each.. $2.90

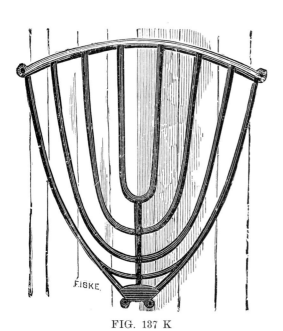

FIG. 137 K

Cast Iron Corner Hay Rack.

Each.. $2.75

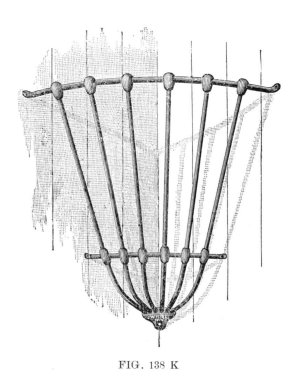

FIG. 138 K

**Wrought Iron Corner Hay Rack, with
Cast Ornaments.**

Each.. $5.00

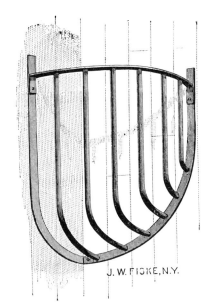

FIG. 139 K   (Left Hand)

Extra Heavy Wrought Iron Corner Hay Rack.

Each... $6.50

With rabbet to receive boards for hay chute, each, net,
   extra.. 1.00

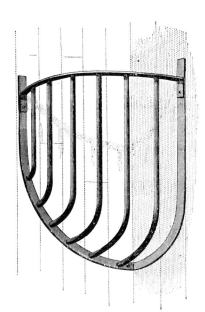

FIG. 140 K   (Right Hand)

Extra Heavy Wrought Iron Corner Hay Rack.

Each... $6.50

With rabbet to receive boards for hay chute, each, net,
   extra.. 1.00

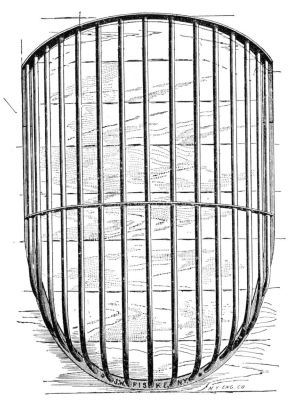

FIG. 141 K

**Wrought Iron Half Circle Hay Rack, extended to do
away with Wood Hay Chute.**

5 feet 6 inches high, each........................... $20.00

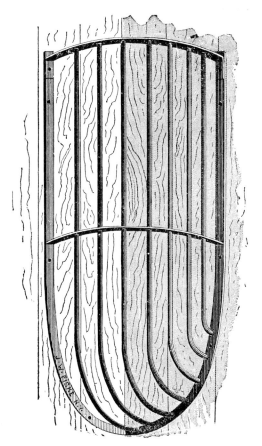

FIG. 142 K

**Wrought Iron Corner Hay Rack, extended to do
away with Wood Hay Chute.**

5 ft. 6 in. high (made both right and left,) each...... $13.00

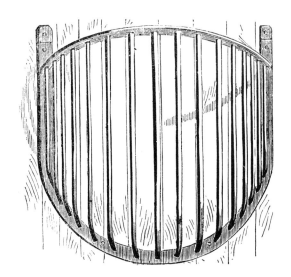

FIG. 143 K

Heavy Wrought Iron Half Circle Hay Rack.

No. 1—42 in. wide, 30 in. high, heavy, each $10.00
"   42   "   30   "   light,   " 8.00
With rabbet to receive boards for hay chute, each, net. 1.50

No. 2—31 in. wide, 24 in. high, each................. 6.00
With rabbet to receive boards for hay chute, each, net. 1.00

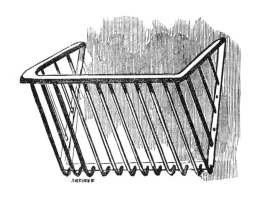

FIG. 144 K

Square Wrought Iron Hay Rack for Centre of Stall.

Each.. $8.00

With rabbet to receive boards for hay chute, each, net,
    extra... $1.00

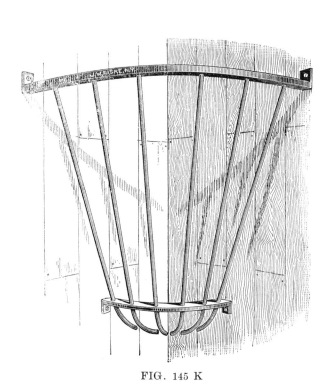

FIG. 145 K

Wrought Iron Corner Hay Rack.

With rabbet to receive boards for hay chute, each.... $4.50
Without rabbet.. 3.50

FIG. 146 K

**Corner Hay Rack, Top and Bottom of Cast Iron,
Uprights of Wrought.**

No. 1—25 in. projection at top, 16 in. at bottom, each.... $3.00
No. 2—18 "   "   "   11 "   "   " 2.75

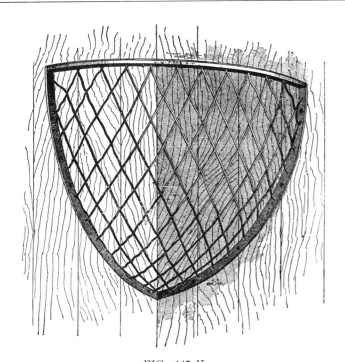

FIG. 147 K

Heavy Wire Corner Hay Rack.

Each $6.00

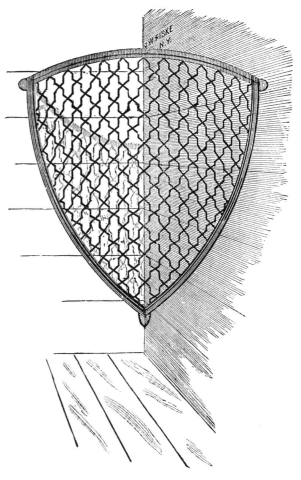

FIG. 148 K

Heavy Wire Corner Hay Rack.

Each... $9.00

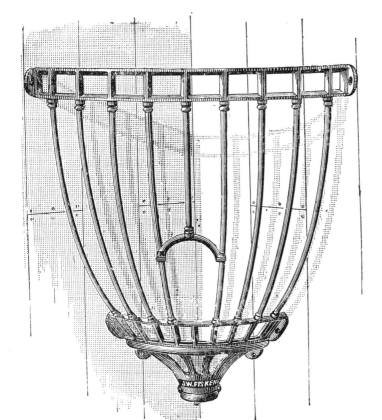

FIG. 149 K

Wrought Iron Hay Rack with Cast Ornaments.

Each.. $8.00

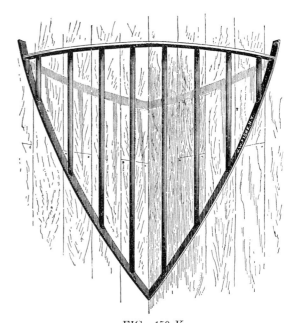

FIG. 150 K

Wrought Iron Corner Hay Rack.

Made with 6 and 8 Bars.

6 Bars, each..$3.00
8 " " 4.00

6 Bars are sufficient and are regularly carried in stock.

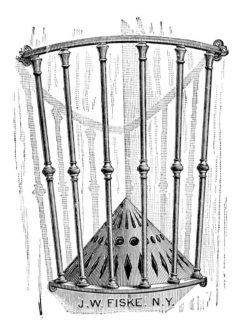

FIG. 151 K

Wrought and Cast Iron Hay Rack with Seed Pan.

Each.................................$6.00

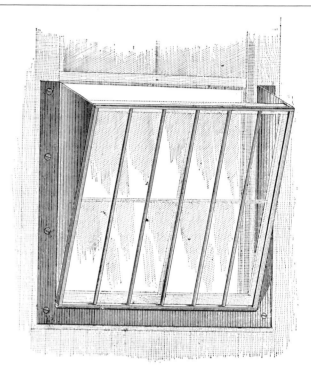

FIG. 152 K

Wrought Iron Window Guard with Side Protectors.

By hanging the window on hinges at bottom, it can be left open without danger of being broken and at the same time preventing a direct draft on the horse.

Side flanges of steel also prevent the frame of window being damaged by horse.

34 inches wide, 30 inches high, including flanges (3 inches wide).................................$7.00

In ordering, give exact inside measurements of guard, allowing for window to swing without striking guard.

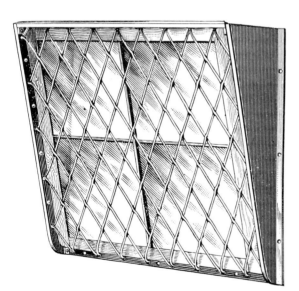

FIG. 153 K

Heavy Wire Window Guard with Side Protectors.

By hanging the window on hinges at bottom, it can be left open without danger of being broken and at the same time preventing a direct draft on the horse.

25 inches wide, 28 inches high, including flanges $6.00

In ordering, give exact inside measurements of guard, allowing for window to swing without striking guard.

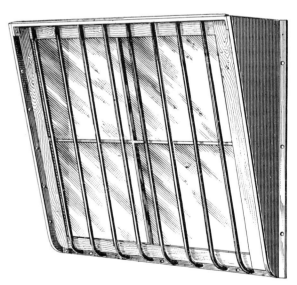

FIG. 154 K

Wrought Iron Window Guard with Side Protectors and Narrow Flange.

Specially adapted for windows in brick buildings.

By hanging the window on hinges at bottom, it can be left open without danger of being broken and at the same time preventing a direct draft on the horse.

34 inches wide, 30 inches high, including flanges........$6.50

In ordering, give exact inside measurements of guard, allowing for window to swing without striking guard.

Any size to order, prices depending on size.

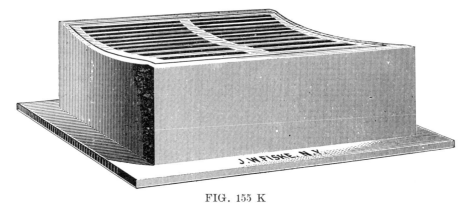

FIG. 155 K

Road Box for Public or Private Roadways, Etc.

Size, 28 inches long, 17½ inches wide, 8 inches deep, each...... ....$14.00
Grating only, each... 5.00

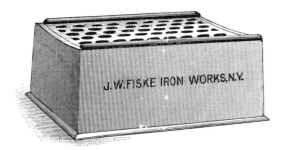

FIG. 156 K

Walk Box for Public or Private Parks, Cemeteries, Etc.

Size, 16½ inches long on top,'9 inches wide, 8 inches deep, each..$6.00
Grating only, 15¾ inches long, 9 inches wide, each........... 2.75

FIG. 157 K

Walk Box for Public or Private Parks, Cemeteries, Etc.

Size, 17 inches long on top, 9 inches wide, 8 inches deep, each..$6.00
Grating only, 15½ inches long, 9 inches wide, each........... 2.75

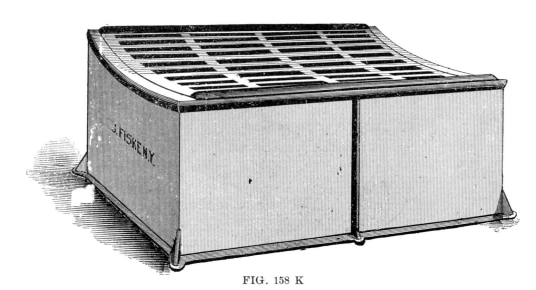

FIG. 158 K

Road Box for Public or Private Roadways, Etc.

No. 1— Size 25 inches long, 14½ inches wide, 10 inches deep, each............................. ....$14.00
No. 2—Size, 32   "   14½   "   4   "   " 11.00
Grating only No. 1—23 inches long, 13¾ inches wide, each...... .... 7.50

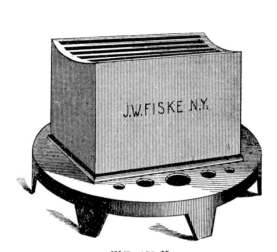

FIG. 159 K

Walk Box.

Size on top, 9 inches long, 6 inches wide, 7½ inches deep:
Total depth, 11 inches, each..... ....$3.00

FIG. 160 K

Silt Vault or Manhole Cover to Set in Stone.

Size, 24 inches diameter, each.............................$6.00
Size, 23 inches diameter, each............................. 5.00

The name of any town or city can be cast on cover.

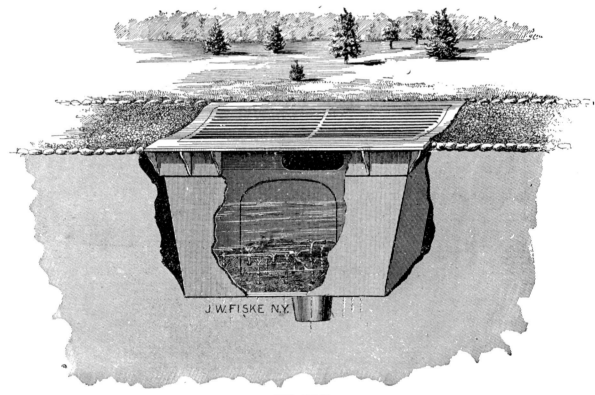

FIG. 161 K

The Weideman Patent Silt for Public and Private Roadways.

Made with movable grating, so that all sediment can be removed by lifting same from bottom of Silt by handle as shown in cut.

This is the most complete Silt in the market and is much cheaper than mason work, and has been adopted in Philadelphia, Washington and other large cities.

Top, 25 inches long, 18¾ inches wide, each...$16.00

FIG. 162 K

Man-hole Frame and Cover.

Frame, 3 inches deep.

No. 1. 12x12 inches, each.................................$ 8.00
No. 2. 18x18 " " 11.00
No. 3. 24x24 " " 15.00

No. 1. Furnished with one handle. Nos. 2 and 3, with two handles.

No. 1 cover, each.....$4.00   No. 2 cover, each.....$7.25
No. 3 cover, each.....$9.50.
Larger sizes made to order.

FIG. 163 K

Man-hole Frame and Cover.

25 inches, diameter of top; 36 inches, diameter of bottom
flange; 9 inches deep, each.......... . ...$21.00
Cover only, 22½ inches diameter, each.... .... 5.00

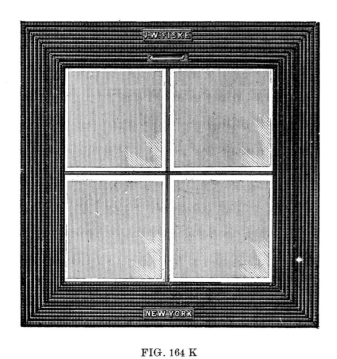

FIG. 164 K

Illuminating Ash-pit Vault Cover, with Frame.

COPYRIGHTED.

Size of Glass, 11½x11½ inches; Frame, 29½x29½ inches,
each.. $12.00

FIG. 165 K

Illuminated Ash-pit Cover, with Rim.

COPYRIGHTED.

27½ inches diameter, including rim; 22½ inches diameter,
without rim, each...................................$14.00

FIG. 166 K

Vault Cover with Rim.

COPYRIGHTED

Extra Heavy.

24 inches diameter, including rim; 18 inches diameter
opening, each......................................$9.00

FIG. 167 K

Water Tight Coal-hole with Rim.

COPYRIGHTED

Extra Heavy Casting.

24 inches diameter, including rim; 18 inches diameter
opening, each.... ....$9.00

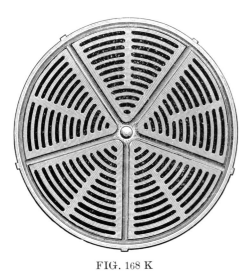

FIG. 168 K

Grating.

Very Heavy.

21 inches diameter, each........................$ 6.00
28   "   "   " 10.00

These gratings are specially adapted for draining
private grounds and will fit in end of soil pipe.

FIG. 169 K

Cesspool Grating with Frame.

24 inches diameter, including frame...........$5.50
Grating only, 21 inches diameter................ 3.50

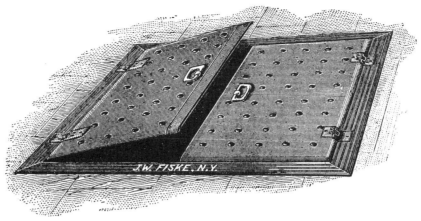

FIG. 170 K

Wrought Iron Manure Pit Door with Cast Iron Frame.

Size of opening, 3x4 feet...$45.00
"   "   4x4   " 50.00
"   "   4x5   " 55.00

FIG. 171 K

Coal-hole Cover, with Rim.

COPYRIGHTED.

16 inches diameter opening, each.................$2.00
20   "   "   including Rim, each......... . 3.25
18   "   " 2.25
22   "   "   including Rim, each.......... 3.75
20   "   " 3.00
24   "   "   including Rim, each.......... 4.75
24   "   " 5.00

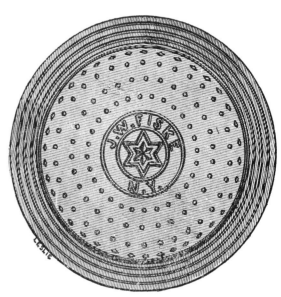

FIG. 172 K

Coal-hole Cover, with Rim.

16 inches diameter, each.........................$1.75
20   "   "   including Rim, each......... 3.00
18   "   " 2.00
22   "   "   including Rim, each......... 3.50
20   "   " 2.50
24   "   "   including Rim, each......... 4.25

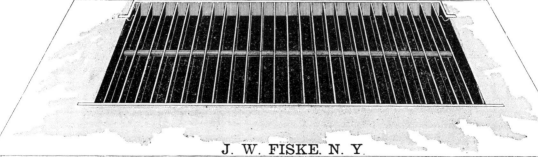

J. W. FISKE. N. Y.

FIG. 173 K

Wrought Iron Grating.

COPYRIGHTED.

Any size made to order.   Estimates and prices given on application.

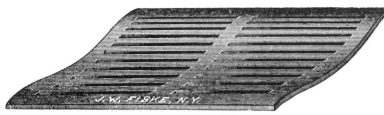

FIG. 174 K

Grating.—Very Heavy.

Especially adapted for public driveways. Size, 21x14¼ inches, each. $5.50

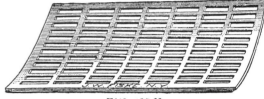

FIG. 175 K

Grating.—Very Heavy.

Especially adapted for driveways in public and private grounds.

Size, 23 inches long, 13½ inches wide, each.....$5.50
"   16   "   "   9   "   " 3.00

FIG. 176 K

Street Gutter Cover.

Any Size and Thickness to Order.

Stock size, 5 ft. 6 in. long, 16 in. wide, 1¼ in. thick, per lineal foot............................... $3.75

Stock size, 4 ft. 6 in. long, 14 in. wide, 1¼ in. thick, per lineal foot........................ .... $3.50

Stock size, 4 ft. long, 16 in. wide, 1½ in. thick, per lineal foot............................ $4.50

Stock size, 4 ft. long, 13 in. wide, 1¾ in. thick, per lineal foot............................ $4.50

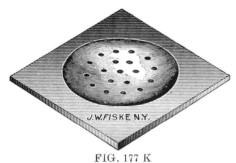

FIG. 177 K

Cesspool Covers.

Size, 10x10 in. each................ ....$ 1.50
"   12x12   "   " 2.00
"   15x15   "   " 3.00
"   20x20   "   " 4.00
"   20x20   "   "   with frame 24x24...   7.00
"   28x28   "   " 10.00

FIG. 178 K

Grating with Frame.

Size, 4x 6 inches on top, each........$1.00
"   8x10   "   "   " 1.50

FIG. 179 K

Oval Grating.

Size, 17¾ inches long, 9¾ inches wide

Each................................$4.00

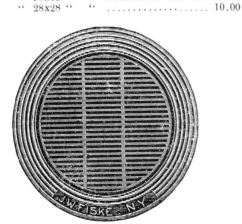

FIG. 180 K

Cesspool Grating with Frame.

For Parks, Private Roadways, etc.

16 inches diameter, not including frame, 22 inches diameter including frame.
Each.........................$4.00
Grating only, 16 in. diameter, each 2.00
"   "   12   "   "   "   1.50
"   "   10   "   "   "   1.00

FIG. 181 K

Round Vault Cover with Glass.

Size, 14 inches diameter, each....$ 3.00
"   16   "   "   " 3.75
"   18   "   "   " 5.50
"   20   "   "   " 8.00
"   24   "   "   " 14.00
"   26   "   "   " 16.00
"   30   "   "   " 24.00
"   36   "   "   " 32.00

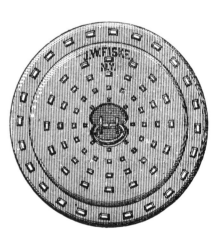

FIG. 182 K

Manure Hole Cover with Frame.

Size, 17 inches diameter, each.....$4.00

FIG. 183 K

Grating with Loose Frame.

Grating 8x8 inches, each................	$0.80
Including frame, "	1.10
Grating 10x10 inches, each....	1.30
Including frame, "	1.70
Grating 13¾x13¾ inches "	1.50
Including frame....................	2.00

FIG. 184 K

Grating.

Size, 9 x 9 inches, each............$1.00
" 13¾ x 13¾ " " $2.00

FIG. 185 K

Cesspool Cover.

5 inches diameter.......	30c
6 " "	35c
8 " "	65c
10 " "	85c
12 " " $1.10

FIG. 186 K

Grating.

Size, 8x 8 inches, each..........$1.25
" 10x10 " " 1.50
" 12x12 " " 1.75

FIG. 187 K

Grating.

Dip, 2½ inches.

6 in. long by 6 in. wide, each........60c
7 " " 6 " " 75c
8 " " 6 " " 85c

FIG. 188 K

Grating.

Dip, 1 inch.

6 in. long by 5 in. wide, each........50c
6 in. long by 5¾ in. wide, each.......60c

Dip, 1¾ inches.

FIG. 189 K

Gratings for Stone or Wood Gutters.

Size, 5x 5 inches, each..........$0.35
" 6x 6 " " .... .40
" 7x 7 " " .... .50
" 5x 8 " " .... .50
" 8x 8 " " .... .75
" 9x 9 " " 1.00
" 8x10 " " 1.00
" 10x10 " " 1.30
" 12x12 " " 1.70

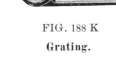

FIG. 190 K

Fresh Air Sidewalk Grating.

Frame, 13½x5¾ inches.

Grating, 11¼x3¾ inches.

Iron, each.....................$ 1.25
Brass, " 12.00

FIG. 191 K

Fresh Air Sidewalk Grating.

Frame 14x5 inches.

Grating, 12x3¼ inches.

Iron, each........ ....$ 1.00
Brass, " 10.00

FIG. 192 K

Grating.

Size, 9½x9½ inches, each..$1.10

FIG. 193 K

Grating.

3 inches diameter..........20c
4 " " 25c
6 " " 35c
6¾ " " 45c
8 " " 70c
9 " " 90c

FIG. 194 K

Manure Pit Frame for Wood Cover.

Outside frame, 1 foot 6 inches by 1 foot 4 inches, each..............$5.00

FIG 195 K

Stall Ventilator.

No. 1, Size, 12x14 inches, each........ .....$3.00
No. 3. "   12x14   "   with back extend-
       ing 3½ inches for brick wall, each...... 5.50

Size of Opening	Black or White Japanned	Gold Bronzed
6 x 8	$1.60	$ 2.10
6 x 10	1.76	2.45
7 x 7	1.60	2 20
7 x 10	1.75	2.70
8 x 8	1.70	2.45
8 x 10	1.75	2.70
8 x 12	1.95	3.00
8 x 15	3.15	4.30
9 x 12	2 25	3.55
9 x 14	2.95	4.30
10 x 10	2.35	3.70
10 x 12	2.55	3.90
10 x 14	2.95	4.40
10 x 16	4.10	5.40
12 x 12	3.75	5.25
12 x 15	4.40	6.40
12 x 17	5.10	7.20
12 x 19	5.85	8.20
14 x 22	8.50	11.50

OPEN

FIG. 196 K

SHUT

FIG. 197 K

Self-indicating Side-wall Registers and Ventilators.

FIG. 198 K

Air Brick with Sliding Ventilator.

Size, 8½x2½ inches, each.................$1.85

FIG. 199 K

Air Brick.

Size, 8½x2½ inches, each............. ...$1.60

FIG. 201 K

Movable Window and Ventilator Combined.

Can be placed directly over the horse's head. allowing a con-
stant blow of fresh air through the stable, with no possibility of
drafts injuring the horses.   Ventilator is easily opened and closed
cr held at any angle.
Size of opening, 2 ft. 11 in. by 20½ in. in center; 14¼ in. at ends.
Size of frame. 3 ft. 4 in. by 2 ft 1 in. in center: 18 in. at ends.

       Each, not glazed...............................$15.00

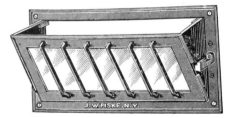

FIG. 200 K

Stall Ventilator with Movable Front.

Size, 16x9½ inches, glazed, each...........$4.00

FIG. 202 K

Round Ventilator.

Size, 8 inches.

Each.......................$1.00

FIG. 203 K

Ventilator.

For Cords.

Each $2.00

FIG. 204 K

Cesspool.

For Wood or Concrete Gutters.

Size, 11x11 inches, each.................$7.00

FIG. 205 K

Cesspool.

For Stable Gutters.

Made Open One or Both Ends.

Size, 11x11 inches, each.................$7.00

FIG. 206 K

Bell Trap Cesspool with Extra Long Spigot.

Size, 10x10 inches, 4 inch outlet, each.... ....$4.50

FIG. 207 K

Bell Trap Cesspool with Extra Long Spigot.

No. 1. 12x12 inch, 4 inches outlet, each $5.00
No. 2. 16x16 "   4 "   "   "   5.50

FIG. 208 K

Box Stall Bell Trap Cesspool with Gutter Branches.

Size of Trap, 12x12 inches; 3 inches outlet, for concrete....$ 9.50
   "   "   12x12   "   3 "   "   " wood floor... 10.50

FIG. 209 K

Bell Trap Cesspool.—Very Heavy.

Size, 12x12 inches, 4 inches outlet, each........$4.00
 "   16x16   "   4 "   "   " 4.50
 "   16x16 in., extra heavy, 4 in. outlet, each.. 6.50

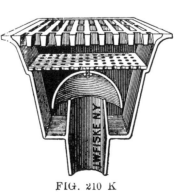

FIG. 210 K

Section View of Fig. 209 K.

Bell Trap Cesspool.

FIG. 211 K

Cesspool.

For Stables, Yards, Etc , with Movable Cover.

Size, 14x18 in , 3 in. outlet, each......$4.00

FIG. 212 K

Bell Trap Cesspool.

Size, 12x12 inches, 3 in. outlet.
Each $4.00
Size, 9x9 inches, 3 in. outlet.
Each..............$3.00
Size, 10x10 inches, 3 in. outlet.
Each..............$3.00
Size, 6x6 inches, 2 in. outlet.
Each..............$1.00

FIG. 213 K

Section view of Fig. 212 K.
Bell Trap Cesspool.

FIG. 214 K

Bell Trap Cesspool.

Size 10x10 inches, 4 inch outlet.

Each..................................$3.75

FIG. 215 K

Bell Trap Cesspool.

Size, 10x10 inches, 4 inch outlet.

Each $5.00

FIG. 216 K

Cesspool.—Extra Heavy.

For Stables, Yards, etc.

Size, 15x15 inches.

4 inch outlet, each. $5.00

FIG. 217 K

Gutter Outlet.

For Concrete or Wood Gutter.

Size, 9¾x8½ inches, each........$2.50

FIG. 218 K

Gutter Outlet.

For Concrete or Wood Gutter.

Size, 7¾x8 inches.

3 inch outlet, each........$3.00

FIG. 219 K

Bell Trap Cesspool.

Size, 8x8 inches.

3 inch outlet, each.....$3.00
Extra heavy, each... $5.00

FIG. 220 K

Bell Trap Cesspool.

For Concrete or Wood Gutter.

Size, 10x10 inches, 4 inch outlet.

Each.................................$3.75

FIG. 221 K

Bell Trap Cesspool.

For Concrete or Wood Gutter.

Size, 7x8 inches, 3 inch outlet.

Each........... .... $3.00

FIG. 222 K

For Concrete or Wood Gutter.

No. 1 Size, 12x12 in., 4 in. outlet, each...$6.00
No. 2 "   13x13 "   4 "   heavy " ... 7.00

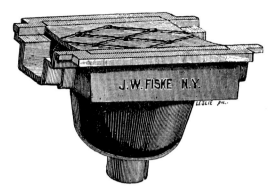

FIG. 223 K

Bell Trap Cesspool.—Very Heavy.

For Fig. 254 K Gutter.

Size, 13x13 inches, 3 inch outlet.

Each..$7.00

FIG. 224 K

Bell Trap Cesspool.

With extra long spigot outlet.

Size, 12½x12½ inches, 4 inch outlet.

Each....................................$6.00

Each. without bell trap........ 5.50

FIG. 225 K

Bell Trap Cesspool.

For Figs. 242 K, 247 K, 249 K, 250 K
and 252 K, Gutter.

Size, 8x8 inches, 3 inch outlet.

Each.............................$4.00

Size, 12x12 inches, 3 inch outlet.

Each.............................$5.00

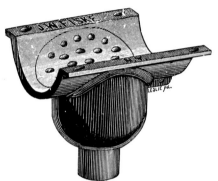

FIG. 226 K

For Concrete or Wood Gutter, also for
Figs. 236 K, 237 K, 238 K, 239 K, and 240 K.

No. 1 Size, 9x9 inches.

Each......................................$3.50

No. 2 Extra heavy, 12½ inches square.

Each.................................. 7.00

FIG. 227 K

Bell Trap Cesspool.

For Figs. 241 K, and 246 K, Gutter.

Size, 12x12 inches, 3 inch outlet.

Each.......................................$5.00

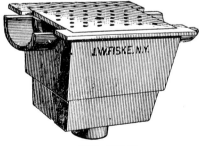

FIG. 228 K

Bell Trap Cesspool.

For Figs. 242 K, 247 K, 249 K, 250 K, and
252 K, Gutter.

Size, 8x8 inches, 3 inch outlet.

Each.................................$4.00

Size, 12x12 inches, 3 inch outlet.

Each.................................$5.00

FIG. 229 K

Section view of Fig. 229 K, Bell Trap
Cesspool.

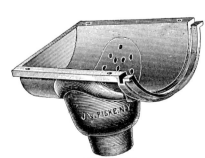

FIG. 230 K

Bell Trap Cesspool.

For Concrete or Wood Gutter, also for
Fig. 251 K, Iron Gutter.

Size, 8x10 inches, 4 inch outlet.

Each..............................$4.00

FIG. 231 K

Gutter Channel.

For level stall floors. By its use the lower floor may be laid level, with the upper flooring laid in opposite direction, parallel with stall channel, which is graded. Can be laid between any width flooring desired.
Each..$1.30

J. W. FISKE, N. Y.

FIG. 232 K

Gutter Channel.

For level stall floors. Graded with flange on either side, 2½ inches over all. Grade commencing at upper end, it grows gradually deeper through the groove.
By using this Gutter Channel, stall floors may be laid level and perfect drainage secured.
From four to five may be used for each open stall as shown in cut Fig. 234 K.
6 feet long, each..$1.25
7 "   "   " 1.50

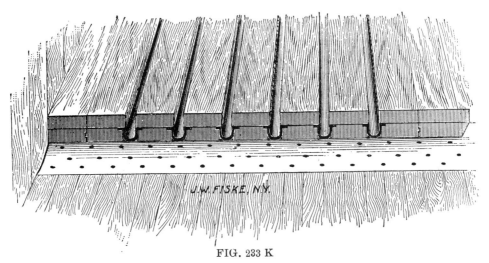

FIG. 233 K

Showing section of open stall, with Gutter Channels draining to main gutter in rear of stall. Any gutter may be used in this connection.

FIG. 234 K

Section of Open Stall with Gutter Channels.

The above illustrates an Open Graded Gutter with separate outlet for each single stall. Furnished in from four feet to four feet six inch lengths. This system combines perfect drainage with a perfectly level floor, care of course being used in laying same.
Set of 4 Graded Gutter Channels, each 5 feet long, and rear gutter 4 feet long, including spigot outlet and closed ends $5.00
Set of 4 Graded Gutter Channels, each 5 feet long, and rear gutter 4 feet 6 inches long. including spigot outlet and closed ends... 6.00
Other sizes made to order if required.

FIG. 235 K

Open Stall Gutter.

Fitted in any length, with or without Traps.

5¼ inches wide, per foot...$0.55
Fig. 226 K, Trap fitted to gutter, extra, each..................................... 3.50
Spigot Outlets, extra, each.. 1.00

FIG. 236 K

Open Stall Gutter.

Fitted in any length, with or without Traps.

7 inches wide, per foot...$0.55
9 "   "   "   " .... .75
Fig. 226 K, Trap fitted to 7 inch gutter, extra, each............................. 3.50
 " 226 K,   "   9   "   "   " 5.50
Spigot Outlets, extra, each.. 1.00

FIG. 237 K

Open Stall Gutter.

Fitted in any length, with or without Traps.

6 inches wide, per foot...$0.80
Fig. 226 K, Trap fitted to gutter, extra, each.................................... 3.50
Spigot Outlets, extra, each.. 1.00

FIG. 238 K

Graded Stall Gutter.

Fitted in any length, with or without Traps.

7 inches wide, graded any length up to 25 feet, per foot.........................$0.65
7 "   "   "   "   " over 25 " up to 40 feet, per foot .... .75
7 "   "   "   "   "   "   40 "   " 55 "   " .... .90
Fig. 226 K, Trap fitted to gutter, extra, each.............................3.50 to 4.00
Spigot Outlets, extra, each.. 1.00

FIG. 239 K

Graded Stall Gutter.

Fitted in any length, with or without Traps.

5¾ inches wide, graded any length up to 25 feet, per foot........................$0.65
5¾ "   "   "   "   " over 25 " up to 44 feet, per foot................... .75
Fig. 226 K, Trap fitted to gutter, extra, each.............................3.50 to 4.00
Spigot Outlets, extra, each.. 1.00

FIG. 240 K

Graded Stall Gutter, with Movable Corrugated Cover for Wood Floor.

Fitted in any length, with or without Traps.

7 inches wide, graded any length up to 20 feet, per foot...$1.40
7 "   "   "   "   over 20 " up to 35 feet, per foot.................................. 1.65
7 "   "   "   "   " 35 " " 50 "   " 2.10
7 "   "   "   "   " 50 " " 70 "   " 2.50
Fig. 228 K, Trap fitted to gutter 12 inches square, each........ .. .. 5.00 to 7.00
Cover only, per foot, (5 inches wide.).. .70

FIG. 241 K

Graded Stall Gutter, with Movable Corrugated Cover for Concrete Floor.

Fitted in any length, with or without Traps.

4½ inches wide, graded any length up to 20 feet, per foot.........................$1.40
4½ "   "   "   "   over 20 " up to 35 feet, per foot................... 1.60
4½ "   "   "   "   " 35 " " 50 "   " 2.00
4½ "   "   "   "   " 50 " " 64 "   " 2.20
Fig. 229 K, Trap fitted to gutter, extra, 8 inches, each........................... 4.00
Fig. 229 K.   "   "   "   " 12   " 5.00
Spigot Outlets, extra, each... 1.00
Cover only, per foot, (3½ inches wide).. .60

FIG. 242 K

Graded Stall Gutter, with Movable Corrugated Cover for Wood Floor.

6 inches wide, graded any length up to 24 feet, per foot...... ....$1.45
6 "   "   "   "   over 24 " up to 40 feet, per foot.................... 1.65
Fig. 229 K, Trap fitted to gutter, extra, 8 inches square, each. 4.00
" 229 K.   "   "   " 12   "   " 5.00
Spigot Outlets, extra, each... 1.00
Cover only, per foot, (3½ inches wide).. .60

FIG. 243 K

Graded Stall Gutter, with Movable Corrugated Cover for Wood Floor.

Fitted in any length, with or without Traps.

8¼ inches wide, graded any length up to 20 feet, per foot........................$1.60
8¼ "   "   "   "   over 20 " up to 30 feet, per foot.................. 1.90
8½ "   "   "   "   " 30 " " 40 "   " 2.30
Fig. 229 K, Trap fitted to gutter, extra, 12 inches square, extra heavy, each.... 7.00
Spigot Outlets, extra, each... 1.00
Cover only, per foot (5½ inches wide).. .70

FIG. 244 K

Graded Gutter, with corrugated Cover for Concrete Floor.

6½ inches wide, graded any length up to 20 feet, per foot........................$1.50
6½ "   "   "   "   over 20 " up to 30 feet, per foot.................. 1.80
6½ "   "   "   "   " 30 " " 40 "   " 2.20
Fig. 229 K, Traps fitted to gutter extra, 12 inches square, extra heavy, each..... 7.00
Spigot Outlets, extra, each 1.00
Cover only, per foot, (5½ inches wide).. .70

FIG. 245 K

Stall Gutter, with Movable Corrugated Cover for Wood Floor.

Fitted in any length, with or withont Traps.

7 inches wide, per lineal foot..$1.20
Fig. 228 K, Trap fitted to gutter, extra, 12 inches square, each..................... 5.00
Spigot Outlet, extra, each... 1.00
Cover only, per foot (5 inches wide).. .70

FIG. 246 K

Stall Gutter, with Movable Corrugated Cover for Concrete Floor.

4½ inches wide, per lineal foot..$1.30
Fig. 229 K, Trap fitted to gutter, extra, 8 inches square, each..................... 4.00
" 229 K, "   "   "   " 12 "   "   " 5.00
Spigot Outlets, extra, each 1.00
Cover only, per foot (3½ inches wide)... .60

FIG. 247 K

Stall Gutter, with Movable Cover for Concrete Floor.

6½ inches wide, per lineal foot...$1.40
Same Gutter, with Flanges for Wood Floor.

8¼ inches wide, per lineal foot..$1.50
Fig. 229 K, Trap fitted to gutter, 12 inches square, extra heavy.................... 7.00
Spigot Outlets, extra, each... 1.00

FIG. 248 K

Stall Gutter, with Movable Corrugated Cover for Wood Floor.

6 inches wide, per lineal foot...$1.35
Fig. 229 K, Trap fitted to gutter, extra, 8 inches square, each..................... 4.00
" 229 K, "   "   "   " 12 "   "   " 5.00
Spigot Outlets, extra, each... 1.00
Cover only, per foot (3½ inches wide)... .60

FIG. 249 K

Stall Gutter, with Movable Corrugated Cover for Concrete Floor.—Very Heavy.

Fitted in any length, with or without Traps.

5 inches wide, per lineal foot...$1.50
Fig. 229 K, Trap fitted to gutter, extra, 12 inches square, each.................... 5.00
Spigot Outlet, extra, each.. 1.00
Cover only, per foot (4 inches wide).. .65

In ordering gutter, please mention where Traps are to be located, and if one or both ends of gutter are to be closed.

FIG. 250 K

Open Stall Gutter.

Fitted in any length, with or without Traps for **Wood Floor.**

8 inches wide, per lineal foot, extra deep..$1.50
Fig. 231 K, Trap fitted to gutter, extra, each...................................... 4.00
Spigot Outlets, extra, each.. 1.00

FIG. 251 K

Stall Gutter, with Cover Screwed On.

6 inches wide, per lineal foot..$1.20
Fig. 229 K, Trap fitted to gutter, extra, 8 inches square, each........................ 4.00
"   229 K,   "   "   "   " 12 "   "   " 5.00
Spigot Outlets, extra, each.. 1.00
Fitted in any length, with or without **Traps.**

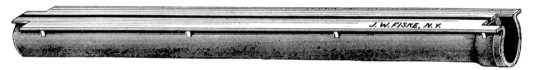

FIG. 252 K

Stall Gutter, with Slit on Top.

6¾ inches wide, per lineal foot, very heavy..$1.50
Bell Trap Cesspool, 12 inches square, each... 5.50

FIG. 253 K

Stall Gutter, with Corrugated Cover.—Very Heavy.

Fitted in any length, with or without Traps.

7 inches wide, per lineal foot...$1.40
Fig. 223 K, Trap fitted to gutter, extra, each...................................... 7.00
Spigot Outlets, extra, each.. 1.00

☞In ordering gutter, please mention where Traps or Spigot Outlets are to be located, and if one or both ends of gutter are to be closed.

FIG. 254 K	FIG. 255 K	FIG. 256 K
T Connection for Fig. 247 K Gutter.	**Right Angle Connection for Fig. 247 K Gutter.**	**Double Right Angle for Fig. 247 K Gutter.**
Each....................$1.25	Each $1.00	Each........................$1.50

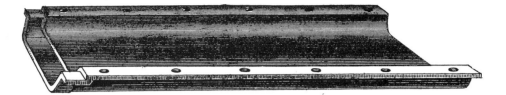

FIG. 257 K

Cow Stable Gutter.

With flanges to screw to floor.

12 inches wide inside, per lineal foot.. ....$1.75
8½ inches wide Inside, per lineal foot 1.60
Trap fitted to gutter, each 7.50

FIG. 258 K

Cow Stable Gutter.

With grating and flanges to screw to floor.

12 inches wide inside, including grating, per lineal foot...................... ....$4.00
        Grating made in 2 feet lengths, and is easily removed.
8½ inches wide inside, per lineal foot............................. .... 3.00

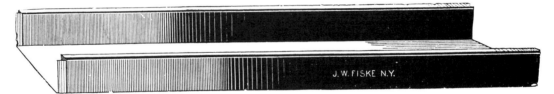

FIG. 259 K

Cow Stable Gutter.

Graded, made any length : 3¼ to 4¼ inches deep.

17 inches wide, per lineal foot.... ....$2.00

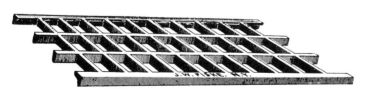

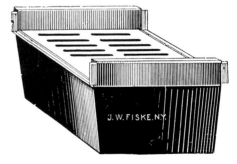

FIG. 260 K

Cast Iron Grating.

For Wood or Concrete Cow Gutters.

Size, 30 in. long, 15 in. wide, per foot............$2.00

FIG. 261 K

Trap.

For Fig. 260 K, Cow Gutter.

Each................................$9.00

☞ In ordering gutter, please mention where Traps or Outlets are to be located. and if one or both ends of gutter are to be closed.

FIG. 262 K

Sanitary Stall Drains.

Design Patented, December 22nd, 1896

No. 1.—5 feet long, 20 inches wide, 4 slats..$15.00   No. 4.—6 feet long, 20 inches wide, 4 slats..$18.00
"   2.—5   "   25   "   5   "   .. 18.00   "   5.—6   "   25   "   5   "   .. 21.00
"   3.—5   "   30   "   6   "   .. 21.00   "   6.—6   "   30   "   6   "   .. 26.00
No. 7.—5 feet long, 30 inches wide, 12 slats..............$22.00

Two No. 2 or No. 3 drains are required for Box Stalls depending on width of Stalls.   See plan, Fig. 265 K, page 78.

Two No. 7 Drains are required for Box Stalls when outlet is in center of Stalls.   See plan, Fig. 269 K, page 80.   Two No. 7 Drains are also used when connected with gutter in rear of range of Stalls.   See plan, Fig. 267 K.

Special graded Gutters ⅛ inch fall to 1 foot with raised bead on each side, one to place under drain to prevent leaking, the other to prevent cement or wood floor from breaking away by the horse's feet.

Per lineal foot, depending on grade and depth of gutter .... $1.50 to $2.25
Bell Trap Cesspools, 8 in. x 8 in., each.......... .... 4.00
"   "   "   12 " x 12 "   " 5.00

When gutter branches from rear gutter into Box Stall, a wider and heavier cover is required and will be charged extra.   See Fig. 265 K page 78.

☞ It will pay you if you expect to build a stable, to remember one thing, this is the only perfect changeable elevated Slat Drain, and will pay for itself in one year.

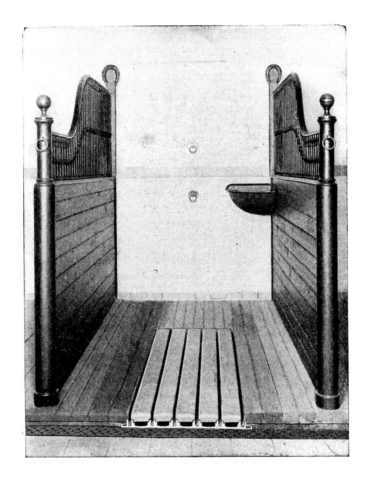

FIG. 263 K

Description of Fiske's Sanitary Stall Drain.

Design Patented, Dec. 22nd, 1896.

Enough has been said regarding the durability, practicability, and necessity of having a perfect Stall Drain, both from a sanitary standpoint and for economy's sake. It is conceded by architects, horse owners, stable keepers, and all interested in the care of horses, that a perfect Drain is necessary in a stable to keep it sweet, clean, and healthy. In order to do this it is important to have a Drain that will carry away all liquid matter, and at the same time economically, to the gutter at rear of stalls.

We wish to call your attention to the advantages of our Drain, which is different from many so called Sanitary Drains in use, being so constructed that the plate can be laid on an almost level floor, obviating the necessity of pitching the stall floor several inches, which is customary, and which horsemen are so much against. By the use of our Drain the horse stands practically level at all times, and not with his feet at an unnatural angle, causing stiffness of joints and straining of the tendons; a grade in the plate, and a slight fall in the floor as well, causes all liquid matter to pass off into the gutter at rear of stalls when in use, and also when stalls are flushed out, which should be often.

Another important feature of our Drain, is that it has a projecting flange extending around three sides of the Drain with a raised bead, which, if properly laid with the stall floor grooved to receive same, should prevent all liquid from leaking through to the floor below. See section views, Figures 271 K, 272 K, and 273 K.

A model of Drain sent on application (loaned) and a sample Drain furnished for approval, if necessary, when 12 or more are wanted.

The slats are so arranged that they do not rest on the bottom of plate, but are raised on parallel ribs or flanges, forming an air space under slats, preventing the slats from absorbing moisture, which evaporating, permeates the atmosphere of the stable, many times causing sickness among horses and ruining the finish on carriages.

The slats are of yellow pitch pine which prevents, to a great extent their absorbing the liquid, as in slats made of other wood. They are also of such a width that the horse has at all times a level space on which to stand.

There are many advantages of a Stall Drain. They are cheaper in the end than any water-tight stall floor that can be made; the slats are easily removed when necessary to wash out or to be replaced by new slats, saving time and labor, as neither nails, screws, nor bolts are used in its construction, the slats being held in place by a simple device.

The Stall Drain will pay for itself in the saving of labor, blankets and straw (bedding) in one year. They are easily put down, and if properly done, need not be removed, simply replacing slats as they become worn out. Slats being movable they can be changed so as to receive an equal amount of wear.

It costs about $8.00 to properly bed one horse a year; by using Fiske's system; the straw saved will soon pay for a Drain.

The gutter at rear of stalls can be of wood, concrete, or iron—iron preferred, as it does not absorb moisture—and, when furnished with a corrugated iron cover, makes a most satisfactory and permanent gutter.

The Drains and Gutter in rear of stalls can be laid either with the Drains raised above the gangway floor or on a level with same. Figs. 263 K, page 74, and 264 K, page 75, and 271 K, page 81, show the Drain in position with the slats above the line of the gangway floor. Figs 272 K, 273 K, and 274 K, page 81, show the Drain with Iron Gutter, the Drain on a level with gangway floor, which some prefer. Fig. 272 K, shows our Drains with corrugated perforated iron cover made in sections, which is removable, and is so arranged on the Drain Plate that the drainage is not interfered with. Fig. 273 K, shows the Drain with Iron Gutter and wood cover, with gangway floor on a level with Drain. Cement gutter can be used in the same way.

It is desirable in Box Stalls to use two Drains, the size of Drain depending on the size of Stall. Fig. 265 K, shows two No. 3 Drains with Iron Gutter grading to front of stall, and, returning, passing in rear of open stalls. Fig. 269 K, shows two No. 7 Box stall Drains with Gutter and separate outlet from Gutter to sewer below. The same plan can be carried out by using Gutter as shown in Fig. 267 K.

Drains and Gutters can be arranged according to architects' plans, suiting any arrangement of stalls.

A narrow Graded Iron Gutter—fall 1-8 inch to the foot—is recommended, giving sufficient pitch and at the same time confining the liquid to a smaller surface than if wide Gutters are used.

The usual care should be taken in laying the Drains and Gutter. Would recommend having the first or lower flooring of stalls made of tongue-and-grooved boards covered with tar paper, or treated with a coating of hot tar or both, under each Drain, to extend well to either side and head of same. Many drains, however, are laid directly on floor beams, using 3 inch yellow pine dressed, for stall floor. The groove in upper floor of stalls should be made to correspond with the beaded flange which projects on three sides of the Drain as shown in the section views, and should be filled with elastic or suitable cement. Give floor of stall a slight pitch which will insure better drainage to Stall and Drain when in use and when flushed out causing all liquid to run into Drain and then into Gutter at rear of stall, which being so slight is not perceptible to the eye and does not affect the horse.

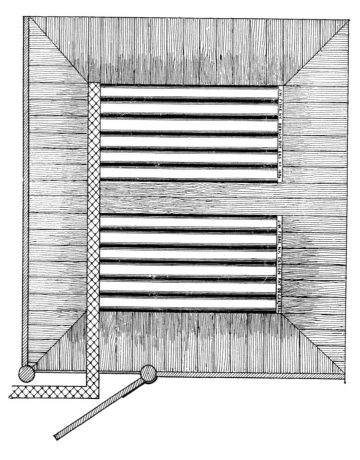

FIG. 264 K

Showing Box Stall with two No. 3 Sanitary Stall Drains and Special Iron Gutter Cover, and
Gutter graded from box stall to main gutter running in
the rear of open stalls.

2 No. 3 Drains, 5 feet x 30 inches, each...$21.00
2 No. 6 "   6 " x 30 "   (for large stall) each 26.00
Special Graded Gutter ⅛ in. fall to 1 ft., depending upon grade and depth of gutter..... ......$1.50 to 2.25
Bell Trap Cesspool, 8 inches by 8 inches, each... 4.00
"   "   "   12 " x 12 "   " 5.00

A special and heavy cover is required for the gutter in Box Stalls as shown in Section, Fig. 266 K
which adds to the cost of gutter in Box Stalls only, per foot................................. .75

Same can be used with concrete floor and gutter.

**Best Drain in use.   Why?   Because it is the most perfect and
every one who sees it says so.**

It contains all the principles of the Original Stall Drain with a number of additional and important features.

A fall toward the Drains should be given to the stall floor at the head and sides of Drains. Also a slight
pitch given to drain to insure better drainage and offset any possible settling of building.

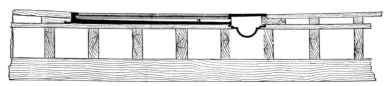

FIG. 265 K

Showing sectional view of two No. 3 Sanitary Stall Drains in position in box stall, with special graded gutter and cover. Same can be used with concrete floor and gutter.

FIG. 266 K

Showing Box Stall with two No. 7 Sanitary Stall Drains, with special iron gutter cover and gutter graded
from box stall to main gutter running in the rear of open stalls.   Same can be
used with concrete floor and gutter.

2 No. 3 Drains, 5 feet x 30 inches, each...$21.00
2 No. 6   "   6   " x 30 "   (for large stalls) each... . 26.00
Special Graded Gutter, ⅛ inch fall to 1 foot, depending upon grade and depth of gutter .....$1.50 to 2.25
Bell Trap Cesspool, 8 inches x 8 inches, each.. 4.00
  "   "   "   12 "   x 12   "   " 5.00
A special and heavy cover is required for the gutter in Box Stalls as shown in Section Fig. 268 K,
    which adds to cost of gutter in Box Stalls only; per foot...................................... .75

**The slats do not rest in the liquid, but are elevated, allowing drainage, and
with air space under slats; a grade is in the casting.**

A fall toward the Drains should be given to the stall floor on all sides of the Drains.
Also a slight pitch given to Drain to insure better drainage and offset any possible settling of building.

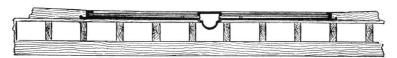

FIG. 267 K

Showing sectional view of two No. 7 Sanitary Stall Drains in position in box stall, with special graded gutter and cover.   Same can be used with concrete floor and gutter.

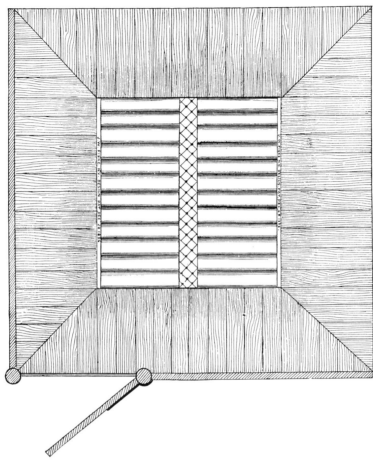

FIG. 268 K

Showing Box Stall with two No. 7 Sanitary Stall Drains, and special iron gutter cover and
graded gutter arranged with separate outlet in center to drain pipe below.

Same can be used with concrete stall floor and gutter.

This plan is recommended as being simplest and best when it is practical to adopt it.

2 No. 7 Drains, 5 feet x 30 inches each, covering space including gutter of 5 feet x 5 feet 6 in , each...$22.00
Graded Gutter for center of stall as shown in Fig. 269 K, grading to outlet in center, with extra heavy
and wide cover, per lineal foot.. . ... 2.25
Drip outlets with grating for center of stall, each.............................. . ... 2.50
Bell Trap, if required, instead of Drip Outlets and Gratings....................... .... 3.50

**The slats are of a proper width and of Yellow Pitch Pine, Mill f̓nished, preventing
to a great extent the absorption of liquid.**

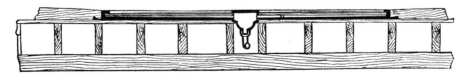

FIG. 269 K

Showing sectional view of two No. 7 Sanitary Stall Drains in position in box stall.   Also showing Iron
Cover and Gutter with separate outlet in center.

Same can be used with concrete stall floor and gutter.

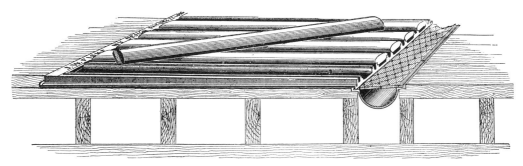

FIG. 270 K

Showing sectional view, in perspective, of Sanitary Stall Drain in position, raised above
the gutter and gangway floor.

The horse stands practically level at all times — a very important item in stall construction.

For prices see Fig. 262 K, page 74.

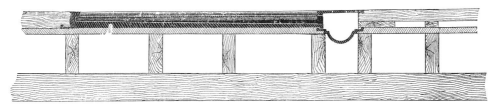

FIG. 271 K

Showing sectional view of Sanitary Stall Drain in position in open stall, on level with gangway floor. with
special iron gutter cover. Same can be used with concrete stall floor and gutter. See Fig. 273 K.

**Our Drain, if properly laid and cared for, will insure a sweet and clean stable. There are no openings
in the channels of our Drain allowing the liquid to run under the slats. We prefer to
confine it to the channels and keep as dry under slats as possible.**

When Iron Cover is used in connection with level gangway floor it should be wider and heavier.
Price per lineal foot for Gutter, including wide cover, depending on grade and depth of gut-
ter. from per lineal foot...... ....$2.25 to $3.50
Bell trap cesspool, 8 inches x 8 inches, each.............................. .... 4.00
  "   "   "   12 "   x 12 "   " 5.00

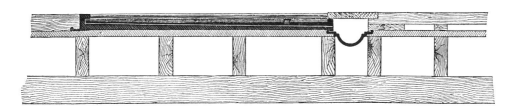

FIG. 272 K

Showing sectional view of Sanitary Stall Drain in position in open stall, on level with gangway floor, with
wooden gutter cover. Same can be used with concrete stall floor and gutter. See Fig. 273 K.

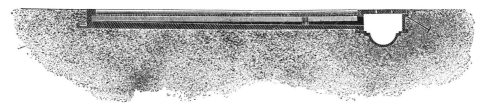

FIG. 273 K

Showing sectional view of Sanitary Stall Drain in position in open stall set in concrete on level with gangway floor, also iron gutter and cover, with special angle piece to anchor into cement
and carry gutter cover, preventing cement from breaking away.

Prices for Gutter, Cover and Traps, same as Fig. 271 K.

Iron Strip with Anchor, to carry Gutter Cover and protecting Concrete, per lineal foot.................60c

Made for both Iron and Wood Cover.

SUGGESTIONS FOR LAYING
FISKE'S SANITARY STALL DRAINS.

There are many ways of securing a tight stable floor, but the following suggestions are given and can be followed when circumstances will permit. Overhauling an old stable and building a new one are two different things, but the same general directions should be followed in order to produce the same result, viz., a substantial and tight floor. It is of course, preferable to calk the stable floor both in stall and passage-way in rear of horses, especially when there is a cellar under the floor or when horses are stabled on second or third floor as is often the case in large cities.

In open stalls when elevated above gangway floor, as in cut Fig. 262 K, which many prefer, as it allows the stablemen to hook out all solid matter from channels between slats on to iron cover of gutter in rear of stalls and easily dispose of it without removing gutter-cover, the liquid draining through holes in cover to gutter underneath:

First—Lay flooring of stall, using 1-inch for bottom and 2-inch on top or 3-inch stuff dressed white-leading joints carefully, giving the floor a fall from the head of stall to gutter, also the sides of stall floor, so water may not remain when stalls are washed out, giving stall perfect drainage and offsetting any possible settling of the building.

Second—Lay iron gutter in place, with white-lead putty, or cement on under side of flanges, which are to be laid in floor, flush with top of same, also leading joints of gutter, bolting same together.

Third—Cover space occupied by Drain Plate thoroughly with a thin coat of asphalt as an extra precaution against leaking. Lay Drain in center of stall with lower end over-hanging lip on edge of gutter flange, first puttying with sufficient quantity of whitelead putty, or elastic cement—vault-light preferred— to guard against leakage.

Fourth—White-lead the joints, and groove out planks next to Drain on sides and upper end to receive raised bead on outer flange of Drain Plate, see cut, Fig. 262 K, filling same with vault-light or suitable cement. Also cut out to form overlap on side flange of outer channel of Drain, thoroughly cementing joint where wood and iron come together.

FOR BOX STALLS.

The same general directions apply to Box Stalls, two Drains being necessary. When using two Drains, other than (No. 7,) it is advisable to place them 9 inches apart as per cut, Fig. 264 K, giving a slight pitch to the floor of stall toward Drains and gutter, as for open stalls.

As it is necessary for gutter cover to be on a level with top of floor, it will also be necessary to rabbet out the floor sufficiently to receive the cover and have slats of Drains 7-8 inch shorter, the cover resting on the channels of Drain on one side and on stall floor on opposite side, as per cut Fig. 265 K.

In using two (No. 7) Drains, they are placed as per cut Fig. 268 K, taking care to pitch sides of stall toward Drain.

When Drains are laid in cement they should be placed in center of stalls as when laid with wood floor, the same care being used to have lip on under side of Drain at foot of stalls overhang projecting bead on flange of gutter.

Gutter can be laid level, as the grade is in the bottom of the gutter, if, however, floor has a slight fall, better drainage of course is obtained.

Give the cement floor of stalls a pitch from all sides of stall to Drain; also give Drain a slight fall, preventing water from remaining when stalls are washed out and to insure better drainage which does not perceptibly affect the standing of the horse.

The following are names of a few who have our drains in use, and to whom we are pleased to refer as to the merits of our Drain.

MRS. MILES STANDISH, ...Stable at Millbrook, N. Y.
WILLIAM H. MENDEL, ...Stable at Mount Vernon, N. Y.
J. F. A. CLARK, ...Stable at Rye, N. Y.
HOWARD TOWNSEND, ...Stable at Southampton, L. I.
J. B. VANDERGRIFT, ...Stable at Lazearville, W. Va.
MRS. E. J. BENTON, ...Stable at Deal Beach, N. J.
CASS LEDYARD, ...Stable in New York City.
GEORGE FOSTER PEABODY, ...Stable in New York City.
PETER F. MEYER. ....Stable at Mamaroneck, N. Y.
AUGUST HECKSCHER, ...Stable at Glen Cove, L. I.
W. McNEIL RODEWALD, ...Stable at Tuxedo Park, N. Y.
JOHN L. RIKER, ...Stable at Long Branch, N. J.
FIRE DEPARTMENT, ...Stable at New Rochelle, N. Y.
A. E. PATTON, ...Stable at Currensville, Pa.
N. F. SICKLES, ...Stable at Mount Vernon, N. Y.
A. D. RUSSELL, ...Stable at Princeton, N. J.
ERNEST FLAGG, Architect, ...Stable at Dongan Hills, S. I.
LEO WISE, ...Stable at Glennville, Conn.
WILLIAM REED, ...Stable in New York City.
J. H. KING, ...Stable at Fair Haven, Conn.
HENRY E. RUSSELL, ...Stable at New London, Conn.
R. J. KIMBALL, ...Stable at Brooklyn, N. Y.
HAMILTON CARY, ...Stable at Westbury, L. I.
GEORGE CLARK, ...Stable at Mamaroneck, L. I.
TROWBRIDGE HOLLISTER, ...Stable at Rutherford, N. J.
R. J. FERRIS, ...Stable at New Rochelle, N. Y.
JUDGE J. M. HALL, ...Stable at New Haven, Conn.
JAMES McLEAN, ...Stable at So. Kortright, N. Y.
GENERAL A. E. BOOTH, ...Stable at Baltimore, Md.
JOHN C. SCOTT, ...Stable at Leesburg, Va.
W. L. BURTON, ...Stable at Woodmere, L. I
MISS ELLEN J. STONE, ...Stable at Ridgefield, Conn.
HENRY P. JANES, ...Stable at Baltimore, Md.
RALPH BARKER, ...Stable at Bridgeport, Conn.
I. GIFFORD LADD. ....Stable at Providence, R. I.
CHARLES M. SCHWAB, ...Stable at Loretto, Pa.
IRA G. PECK, ...Stable at Hartford, Ct.
WARREN D. HOBBS, ...Stable at No. Grafton, Mass
HON. THOMAS F. WALSH, ...Stable at Washington, D. C.
CHARLES E. FORD, ...Stable at Baltimore, Md.
R. H. McLANE, ...Stable at Millbrook, N. Y.
HELLMAN BREWING CO., ...Stable at Waterbury, Conn.
F. P. MOORE, ...Stable at Glen Cove, L. I.
D. FAIRFAX BUSH, ...Stable at Glen Cove, L. I.
C. ADOLPHE LOW, ...Stable at Sharon, Conn.
JAY G. CARLISLE, ...Stable at Brooklyn, N. Y.
R. G. KIMBALL, ...Stable at Brooklyn, N. Y.
WINTHROP BURR, ...Stable at Lawrence, L. I.
C. K. G. BILLINGS, ...Stable at Washington Heights, N. Y.
R. D. WINTHROP. ....Stable at Roslyn, L. I.
CHARLES E. DIEFENTHALER, ...Stable at New Canaan, Conn.
DR. G. M. TUTTLE, ...Stable in New York City.
HENRY J. HARTENBURGH, ...Stable at Bernardsville, N. J.
LUTHER KOUNTZE, ...Stable at Morristown, N. J.
THOS. HASTINGS, ...Stable at Port Washington, L. I.
M. H. BEERS, ...Stable at Far Rockaway, L. I.
F. R. JOHNSON, ...Stable at Ansonia, Conn.
C F. SLAYBACK, ...Stable at Montclair, N. J.
H. S. JULIA, ...Stable at Mount Kisco, N. Y.
J. K. BRANCH, ...Stable at Pawling, N. Y.
PATRICK GARVAN, ...Stable at Hartford, Conn.

HON. W. C. WHITNEY, ...Stable at Aiken, S. C.
W. E. CONNOR, ...Stable at Seabright, N. J.
LAFLIN KELLOGG, ...Stable in New York City.
W. E. TAILER, ...Stable in New York City.
E. A. DARLING, ...Stable at Lyndonville, Vt.
M. C. LEFFERTS, ...Stable at Cedarhurst, L. I.
E. L. TYLER, ...Stable at Anniston, Ala.
MAXWELL EVARTS, ...Stable at Windsor, Vt.
SELMAR HESS, ...Stable at Long Branch, N. J.
W. B. BOLTON, ...Stable at Lawrence, L. I.
ISAAC MILBANK, ...Stable at Portchester, N. Y.
W. E. ASIEL, ...Stable at Elberon, N. J.
W. C. BROWNING, ...Stable at Alexandria Bay, N. Y.
W. W. & T. M. HALL, Builders, ...Stable in New York City.
W. K. CROMWELL, ...Stable in Baltimore, Md.
A. L. CROSS, ...Stable at Montclair, N. J.
H. J. LAMARCHE, ...Stable at Locust Point, N. J.
W. CHILDS, JR., ...Stable at Bernardsville, N. J.
M. HELLYER, ...Stable at Rockville Centre, L. I.
S. UHLMANN, ...Stable at Cooperstown, N. Y.
HOWARD WILLETTS, ...Stable at White Plains, N. Y.
WM. G. ROCKEFELLER, ...Stable at Greenwich, Conn.
MRS. E. W. BLISS, ...Stable at Cooperstown, N. Y.
C. WEISBECKER & CO., ...Stable in New York City.
C. A. WINCH ICE COMPANY, ...Stable in New York City.
JAMES CHESTERMAN, ...Stable at Valati, N. Y.
BRAYTON IVES,.. ....Stable at Scarborough, N. Y.
RUDOLPH H. KESSEL, ...Stable at Morristown, N. J.
ROBT. A. McCURDY, ...Stable at Morris Plains, N. J.
R. W. TAILER, ...Stable in New York City.
W. W. CONDE, ...Stable at Watertown, N. Y.
WEST ORANGE FIRE DEPARTMENT, ...Stable at West Orange, N. J.
DAVENPORT WATER COMPANY, ...Stable at Davenport, Iowa.
JOHN J. MOORE, ...Stable in New York City.
L. A. THEBAUD, ...Stable at Morris Plains, N. J.
O. C. FARRIS, ...Stable at Morris Plains, N. J.
MRS. STEPHEN WHITNEY, ...Stable at Morris Plains, N. J.
R. C. VRIT, ...Stable at Atlantic Highlands, N. J.
E. H. NICHOLS, ...Stable at Boston, Mass.
DR. WALTER B. JAMES, ...Stable at Cold Spring Harbor, L. I.
THE JOHN KRESS BREWING COMPANY..Stables in New York City.
W. A. BLOODGOOD, ...Stable at Seabright, N. J.
JASPER LYNCH, ...Stable at Lakewood, N. J.
S. S. SPAULDING, ...Stable at Richfield Springs, N. Y.
SOLOMON LOEB, ...Stable at Seabright, N. J.
C. LEDYARD BLAIR, ...Stable at Far Hills, N. J.
SPENCER TRASK, ...Stable at Saratoga Springs, N. Y.
S. QUACKENBUSH, ...Stable at East Hampton, L. I.
GEO. REED, ...Stable in New York City.
MRS. ALFRED CORNING CLARK, (Mrs. Henry C. Potter),..Stable in New York City.
D. CRAWFORD CLARK, ...Stable at Essex, N. Y.
F. H. DAVIES, ...Stable in East Hampton, L. I.
DR. J. E. BOWMAN, ...Stable at Geenwich, Conn.
CHAS. L. HENRY, ...Stable in Anderson, Ind.
T. P. FISKE, ...Stable at Westbrook, Conn.
LeGRAND L. BENEDICT, ...Stable at Cedarhurst, L. I.
A. M. GREER, ...Stable at Larchmont, N. Y.
NELSON PERRIN, ...Stable at Baltimore, Md.
JOHN A. McCALL, ...Stable at Long Branch, N. J.
W. R. KUHN, ...Stable at Pittsburg, Pa.
ISAAC KAUFMAN, ...Stable at Pittsburg, Pa.
E. H. SHEARSON, ...Stable at Greenwich, Conn.
GEORGE LAUDER, ...Stable at Greenwich, Conn.
WM. TRUSLOW HYDE, ...Stable at Greenwich, Conn.
ALLAN McLANE, ...Stable at Baltimore, Md.
GEO. J. CAPEWELL, ...Stable at Hartford, Conn.

FIG. 274 K

Improved Sanitary Stall Drain.—Pan System.

Patent Applied for April, 1898.
Patent Granted, 1899.

In placing Pan Drains in single stalls, they should project 5 inches beyond the line of stall posts.

No. 8.   6 feet long, 21 inches wide, 4 slats...$20.00
No. 9.   6 feet long, 26 inches wide, 5 slats.. 23.00
No. 10. 6 feet long, 31 inches wide, 6 slats.. 27.00
No. 11. 5 feet x 5 feet, 12 slats, for Box Stalls... 41.00

The above prices include Slats and Bell=Trap.

No rear gutter is required with this system, saving from $5.00 to $7.00 per single stall.

DESCRIPTION OF FISKE'S SANITARY STALL DRAIN,
PAN SYSTEM.

We have previously mentioned the importance and necessity of having a perfect Drainage System in stables, and have called attention to the important points of our movable elevated slat Drain, which has met with approval among architects, owners and horsemen generally, on account of its practical points, which are not found in any other drain. We now wish to call your attention to an improvement, in what is known as The Solid Pan Drain, which many have used and like, and some prefer. To supply this demand we have designed and wish to call special attention to our patent Pan Drain which is in one casting with bell trap in center, a little to the rear, the four sides of the Drain grade to the trap, allowing all liquid matter to pass off quickly, through trap, to sewer pipe under stable floor, doing away entirely with a rear gutter.

The top of Drain, being level with floor of stall, is also flush with gangway floor, so that the horse stands level at all times.

The slats which are mill finished of pitch pine, prevent to a great extent the absorption of moisture, are removable and interchangeable, so that the slats can not only be changed from one position in Drain to another allowing an even wearing of the slats, but they are reversible and can also be turned end for end, so that both sides and ends of slats may receive equal use, a very important item in the economy of stall floors; they are easily removed, allowing the attendant an opportunity to clean out often any solid matter that may work through the slats, which can be kept practically clean by use of a stall hook, by simply passing between the slats, which on account of the construction of Drain, can be drawn, unobstructed, the entire length. The slats are held in place, and are prevented from being misplaced while in use, by a simple device as shown in illustration, Fig. 274 K, which not only holds the slats in place, but allows them to be reversed. The slats have a bearing at both ends of drain, also upon beveled uprights, properly spaced, and which are cast to the bottom of the pan.

Those preferring a Pan Drainage System will find in this Drain the most simple, economical and perfect Drain on the market. No bolts, nails or screws are a part of its construction; no hinges to rust, wear out, or break off; no heavy trap door (grating) to open; no wrought iron carriage bars to rust out and secrete foul liquid matter; but a simple, practically unobstructed Drain which is easily kept clean by broom or hose, and when not convenient a few pails of water is all that is necessary.

For box stalls, the same plan is adopted, only a larger Drain is required viz: 5 ft. x 5 ft., which for stalls of ordinary size, when finished, leave a margin of from 1 ft. 6 in. to 2 ft. 6 in. on the four sides of Drain, see Fig. 278 K.

SUGGESTIONS FOR LAYING PAN DRAIN.

The same general suggestions apply to laying Fiske's Pan Drain as are given for our movable elevated slat Drain, care to be taken to prevent leakage of joints between the Drain and stall floor, which, if properly cemented or otherwise prepared, no leakage can occur. The flange projecting around the four sides of the Drain, both for box and open stalls, as shown in Fig. 275 K, should prevent leakage.

For Simplicity and Economy, Use Fiske's System of Drainage.

The following are the names of a few who have Pan Drains in use and to whom we are pleased to refer as to the merits of our Pan Drain.

EDGAR L. ROPKINS, ...Stable in Hartford, Conn.
E. H. HARRIMAN, ...Stable in New York City.
J. T. SAFFEN, ...Stable at Pelham Manor, N. Y.
JAMES H. HYDE, ...Stable at Bayshore, L. I.
JAMES H. HYDE, ...Stable in New York City.
MOSES TAYLOR, ...Stable at Mount Kisco, N. Y.
WILLIAM A. ENGEMAN, ...Stable at Brooklyn, N. Y.
MISS HELEN M. GOULD, ...Stable in New York City.
R. D. WINTHROP, ...Stable in New York City.
MRS. ALFRED CORNING CLARK, (Mrs. Henry C. Potter)...Stable at Cooperstown, N. Y.
FRANK J. GOULD, ...Stable at Irvington-on-Hudson, N. Y.
FRANK J. GOULD, ...Stable in New York City.
FIRE DEPARTMENT, ...Stable at Trenton, N. J.
FIRE DEPARTMENT, ...Stable at Summit, N. J.
FIRE DEPARTMENT, ...Stable at New Rochelle, N. Y.
WARREN DELANO, JR., ...Stable at Barrytown, N. Y.
BENEDICT & BURNHAM MFG. CO.,...Stable at Waterbury, Conn.
JANEY, SEMPLE, HILL & CO., ...Stable at Minneapolis, Minn.
JOHN HARRIGAN, ...Stable at Albany, N. Y.
HON. T. W. PHILLIPS, ...Stable at New Castle, Pa.
GEO. W. DIBBLE, ...Stable at Mount Vernon, N. Y.
RALPH BARKER, ...Stable at Bridgeport, Conn.
F. T. F. LOVEJOY, ...Stable at Pittsburg, Pa.
H. W. CROFT, ...Stable at Pittsburg, Pa.
MRS. MARY C. THAW, ...Stable at Pittsburg, Pa.
COL. R. H. I. GODDARD, ...Stable at East Greenwich, Conn.
COL. O. H. PAYNE, ...Stable at Thomasville, Ga.
JACOB KAUFMANN, ...Stable at Allegheny, Pa.
J. V. THOMPSON, ...Stable at Uniontown, Pa.
F. M. SEMANS, JR., ...Stable at Uniontown, Pa.
T. N. BARNSDALL, ...Stable at Pittsburg, Pa.
G. H. STAPELY, ...Stable at Cincinnati, Ohio.
L. C. PHIPPS, ...Stable at Pittsburg, Pa.
J. B. EISMAN, ...Stable at Pittsburg, Pa.
R. B. LITTLE COMPANY, ...Stable at Providence, R. I.
J. R. HAMILTON, ...Stable at Allegheny, Pa.

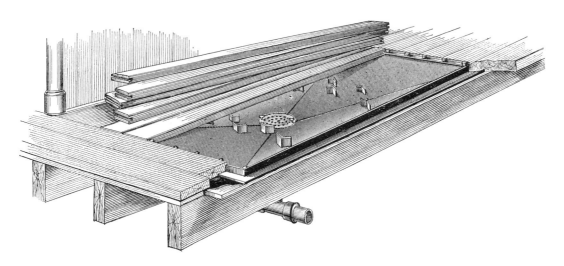

FIG. 275 K

Showing Sanitary Pan Drain in position in Single Stall with 4 slats removed, exposing to view interior of pan, slat supports, mode of securing slats, also trap outlet, being on a level with Stall and Gangway floor.

☞In placing Pan Drain in position, have rear of Drain project 5 inches beyond line of posts.

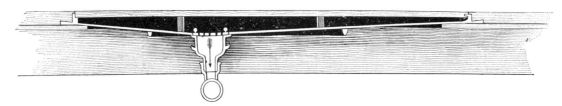

FIG. 276 K

Showing Sectional View (lengthwise) of Sanitary Pan Drain in position in Single Stall, being on a level with Stall and Gangway floor.

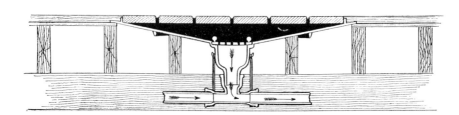

FIG. 277 K

Showing Cross Section of Sanitary Pan Drain in position in Single Stall, being on a level with Stall and Gangway floor.

Drains can be used in connection with Wood, Brick or Concrete Stall Floor.

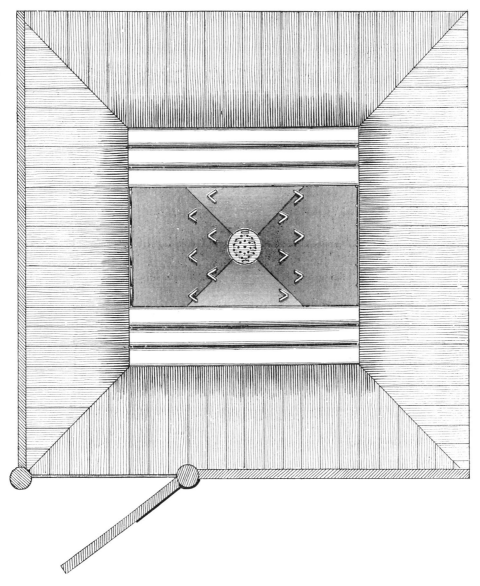

FIG. 278 K

Showing Sanitary Pan Drain in position in Box Stall with 6 slats removed, exposing to view interior of pan, slat supports, mode of securing slats, also trap outlet.

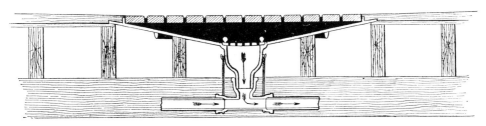

FIG. 279 K

Showing cross section of Pan Drain in position in Box Stall, being level on top, sides slightly graded to Drain.

Drains can be used in connection with Wood, Brick or Concrete stall floor.

FIG. 280 K

Hog Trough, with Division for Water.

```
Size, 3 feet long, each.................................................................$4.75
  "   4   "      "   .................................................................. 5.00
  "   5   "      "   .................................................................. 6.50
```

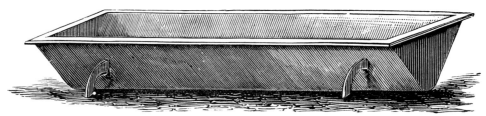

FIG. 281 K

Hog Trough.

```
Size, 3 feet long, each...............................................................$4.50
  "   3 feet 6 inches long, each..................................................... 5.00
  "   4 feet long, each................................................................ 5.50
  "   4 feet 6 inches long, each...................................................... 6.00
  "   5 feet long, each................................................................ 6.50
  "   6 feet long, each................................................................ 7.50
```

FIG. 282 K

Hog Trough, with Division for Water.

```
Size, 4 feet long, each...............................................................$6.50
  "   5   "      "   .................................................................. 7.50
  "   6   "      "   .................................................................. 8.50
```

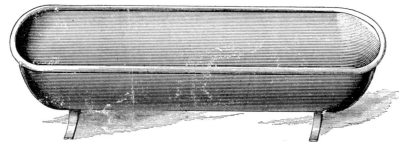

FIG. 283 K

Hog Trough.

```
Size, 3 feet long, each...............................................................$3.75
  "   4   "      "   .................................................................. 4.50
  "   5   "      "   .................................................................. 5.50
```

Any of the above can be galvanized to order.

FIG. 284 K

Showing Salt Brick and Feeder
in Cow Stable.

FIG. 285 K

Salt Brick and Feeder.

In use in all up-to-date stables.

Provide pure, fine salt for both Horses
and Cattle. They will do better and
keep healthy.

Salt Brick, each, net................25c
Gal. Iron Feeders, each, net 50c

FIG. 286 K

Showing Salt Brick and Feeder
in Horse Stable.

FIG 287 K

Cow Manger.

40 inches long, 24 inches wide.

Each....................................$14.00

FIG. 288 K

Dog Trough.

For Food and Water.

18 in. long, 6 in. wide, 4½ in. deep, each....$2.50

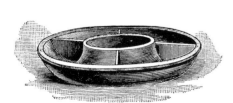

FIG. 289 K

Poultry Trough.

For Food and Water.

16 inches diameter, each..........$3.00

FIG. 290 K

Cow Trough or Manger.

7 feet long, 20 inches wide on top, 9 inches deep in front, 14 inches deep at back.

Each..$27.00

FIG. 291 K. No. 2.

Automatic Watering Device.

Same as Fig. 292 K, No. 3, except valve is raised in center of Basin instead of being flush with bottom of Basin as in Fig. 292 K, No. 3.

Each $1.75

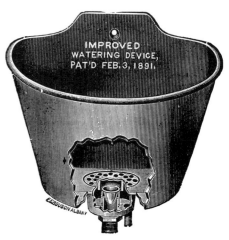

FIG. 292 K. No. 3.

Automati Watering Device, Improved Style.

12x18 inches on top, 9 inches deep.
Weighing 20 lbs. and holding from three to three and one-half gallons.

Never wears out. The water is always before the stock. Water is of same temperature as stable. Saves feed, prevents the spread of disease and increases the quantity of milk 10 to 20 per cent. Iron basins are sweet and clean, the check valve in bottom of basin prevents clogging of pipes.

Are easily put up and will pay for themselves in a short time.

Each...... ....$2.00

FIG. 293 K

Showing Watering Devices in place, also Supply Pipe and Governing Tank, which must be placed on a line with the Basin.

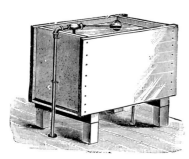

FIG. 294 K

Supply or Governing Tank.

Can be made of Wood or Galvanized Iron.

Galvanized Iron Tank, 24 inches long, 12 inches wide, 18 inches deep, including Ball and Valve for ¾ inch pipe.

Each.. ......$5.00

FIG 295 K

Box Stall Watering Device.

15 inches long, 8 inches wide, 6 inches deep.

Each.. ....$1.75

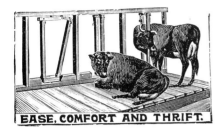

FIG. 296 K

Swinging Cattle Stanchion.

Price, each............................ ....$1.75

Adjusts itself when open, so that the animal cannot turn it when backing out, and locks itself when closed, giving perfect freedom, allowing the head to turn either side, thus enabling them to lick their shoulders, drive off flies and lie down with ease.

They are strong and durable, and not liable to get out of order.

When closed, the cattle cannot unlock them. Any carpenter can put them up. To close them, simply press on the side piece and it locks itself.

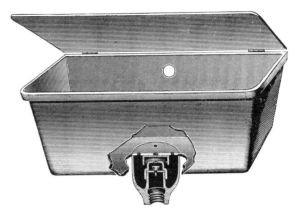

FIG. 297 K

Woodward's Patent Cow Watering Device

Made with and without covers.

Basin, with Strainer and Trap, including Valve and Seat, as shown
in cut, each..$2.75
Covers, each, extra 1.00

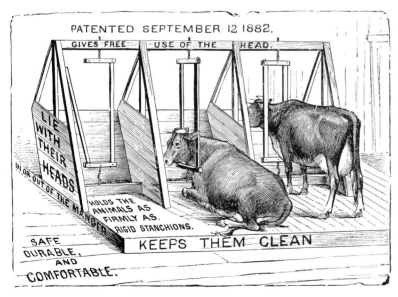

FIG. 298 K.

Chain Hanging Cattle Stanchion.

Giving perfect freedom and comfort.

Young Stock size, 5½ inches neck space................$2.00
Cow size, 6½ and 7 inches neck space 2.00
Ox or Steer size, 9 and 10 inches neck space 2.50
Heavy Bull size, 11 and 12 inches neck space 3.00

Make the bottom sill of 4 x 4 inch timber, with top edge 7 inches from floor; exactly 4 feet and 4 inches above the top edge of the bottom sill place a 4 x 4 inch timber; bore an inch hole in bottom sill 3 inches deep in center of stall; bore a ⅜ inch hole crossways of bottom sill 2 inches from top edge, passing through the inch hole; bore a ⅜ inch hole through the top timber on line with the first hole; take the fastener and pass the eye-bolt through the ⅜ inch hole in top timber; place the washer on top side of timber and then turn nut tight; insert chain in inch hole in the bottom sill, pass the 4½ inch bolt through ⅜ inch hole and first link of chain and turn nut tight; cut a slot in partition to receive arm and the fastener is ready for use.

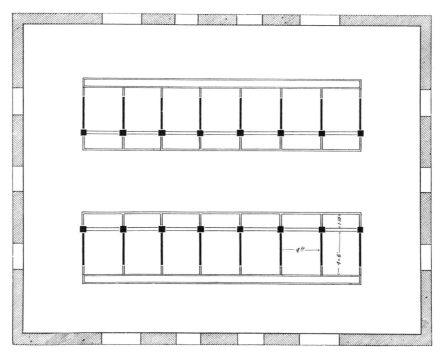

Interior Ground Plan of Cattle House.

FIG. 299 K

Showing 2 ranges of 7 stalls each including rear gutter, with passages.   Stalls laid out for
fixtures as shown in Fig. 300 K.

FIG. 300 K

Showing Cow Stall fitted with Iron Ramps, Sill and Cap Rails, Tie Bars, etc., arranged for both
Wood and Iron Posts. See Fig. 301 K and 302 K, page 95.

☞ Prices on above fittings given upon application.

☞ We also make a cast iron ramp and partition in one piece also division between heads of cattle, price given upon application.

FIG. 301 K

Showing two Ranges of Cow stalls fitted with Iron Posts, Ramp and Sill Rails, Gutter, etc.

☞Prices given upon application.

FIG. 302 K

SHOWING A RANGE OF COW STALLS FITTED UP WITH
OUR IMPROVED IRON FITTINGS.

COW STABLE OF

D. WILLIS JAMES, Esq.

MADISON N. J.

FIG. 303 K

Showing Two Ranges of Cow Stalls.

Arranged with passage between for feeding.

Post, each.... ....$10.00 | Manger for two cows, 7 feet. each............$27.00
Gutter, per lineal foot $1.75
Cap and Sill Rail, per lineal foot, each... ....$1.25

FIG. 304 K

SHOWING A RANGE OF COW STALLS FITTED UP WITH   COW STABLE OF
OUR IMPROVED IRON FITTINGS.   H. McKAY TWOMBLY, Esq.,
                                                  MADISON, N. J.

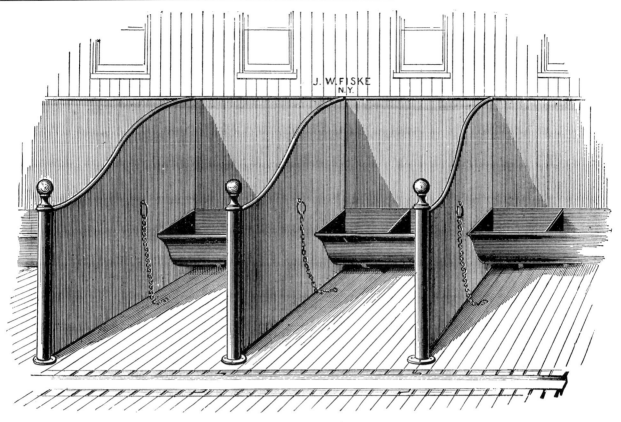

FIG. 305 K

Showing Three Cow Stalls.

Stall Posts, each.....................................$12.00	Tying Chains, each...............................$ 0.75
Ramp Rails, each................................. 5.50	Gutter, per lineal foot...................... .... 1.75
Bottom Rails, each............................. 4.00	Manger for two Cows........................... 27.00

Stall partitions 4 feet high at post. running to 5 feet 6 inches high at head of stalls, which
are 7 feet wide, accommodating 2 Cows.

FIG. 306 K

Showing Range of Open and Box Cow Stalls, fitted up with Iron Ramp, Cap and Sill Rails,
Gutter, Tie Bars, etc.

As used in many of our Modern Cow Stables.

See cut, Fig. 300 K, page 94, showing single stall on larger scale.

Prices given upon application.

FIG. 307 K

Box Stall Post and Column Combined.

5½ inch diameter, 12 ft. 6 in. high.

Each.................$45.00

J.W. FISKE
NEW YORK

FIG. 308 K

Stall Post.

5½ inches diameter,
6 feet high.

Each.........$17.00

FIG. 309 K

Box Stall Post.

5½ inches diameter.
7 ft. 6 in. high.

Each.........$18.00

8 feet high.

Each.........$19.00

FIG. 310 K

Stall Post.

5 inches diameter,
6 ft. 3 in. high.

Each......$15.00

7 ft. 9 in. high

Each......$19.00

FIG. 311 K

Stall Post and Column Combined.

5 inches diameter.
Any height made to order.

Per foot.................$2.25

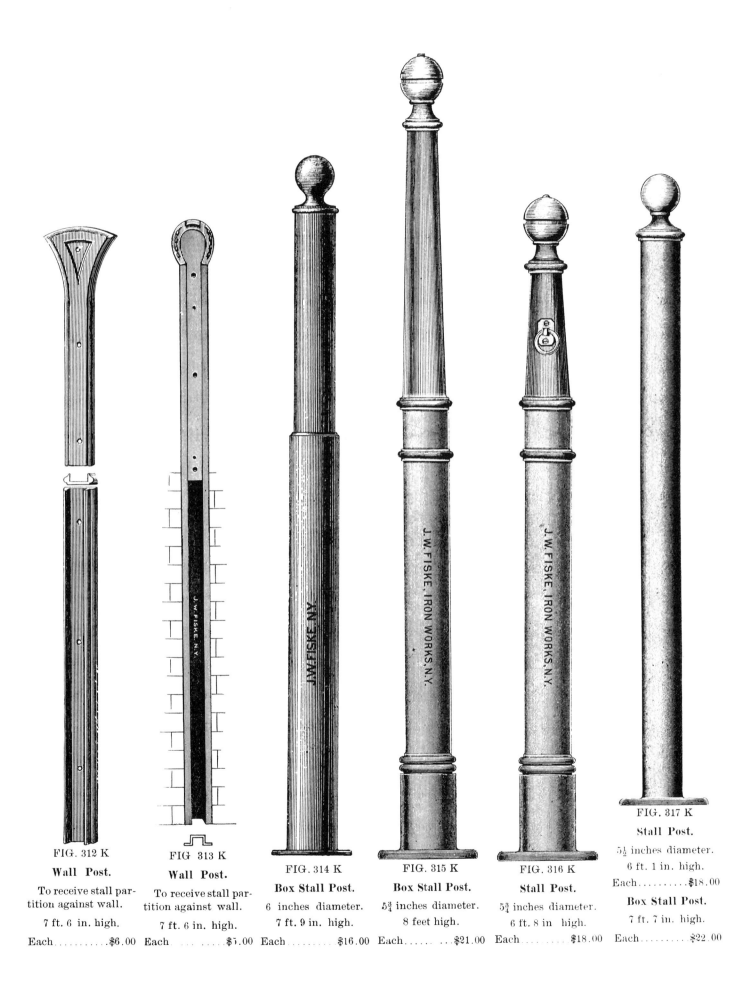

FIG. 312 K
Wall Post.
To receive stall par-
tition against wall.
7 ft. 6 in. high.
Each..........$6.00

FIG 313 K
Wall Post.
To receive stall par-
tition against wall.
7 ft. 6 in. high.
Each..........$5.00

FIG. 314 K
Box Stall Post.
6 inches diameter.
7 ft. 9 in. high.
Each..........$16.00

FIG. 315 K
Box Stall Post.
5¾ inches diameter.
8 feet high.
Each..........$21.00

FIG. 316 K
Stall Post.
5¾ inches diameter.
6 ft. 8 in high.
Each..........$18.00

FIG. 317 K
Stall Post.
5½ inches diameter.
6 ft. 1 in. high.
Each..........$18.00
Box Stall Post.
7 ft. 7 in. high.
Each..........$22.00

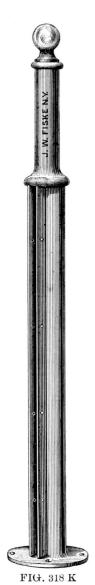

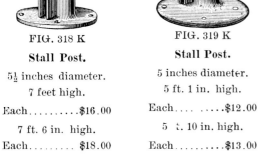

FIG. 318 K

Stall Post.

5½ inches diameter.

7 feet high.

Each..........$16.00

7 ft. 6 in. high.

Each..........$18.00

FIG. 319 K

Stall Post.

5 inches diameter.

5 ft. 1 in. high.

Each...........$12.00

5 ft. 10 in. high.

Each..........$13.00

FIG. 320 K

Square Stall Post.

5 inches square.

6 ft. 2 in. high.

Each.........$20.00

Box Stall Post.

7 ft. 6 in. high.

Each.........$24.00

FIG. 321 K

Stall Post.

To set in concrete.

5 inches diameter.

6 ft. 8 in. high.

Each..........$15.00

Box Stall Post.

9 feet high.

Each..........$19.00

FIG. 322 K

Stall Post.

To Set in concrete.

7 ft. 6 in. high.

4⅝ in. diam.

Each.......**$16.00**

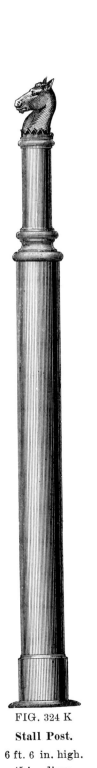

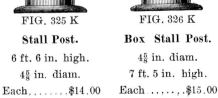

FIG. 323 K

Square Stall Post.

For fronts of Box Stalls as shown in Fig. 62 K.

Prices given upon application.

FIG. 324 K

Stall Post.

6 ft. 6 in. high.

4⅝ in. diam.

Each.......$15.00

FIG. 325 K

Stall Post.

6 ft. 6 in. high.

4⅝ in. diam.

Each........$14.00

FIG. 326 K

Box Stall Post.

4⅝ in. diam.

7 ft. 5 in. high.

Each......,.$15.00

FIG. 327 K

Stall Post.

6 ft. 6 in. high.

5 in. diam.

Each.......$26.00

Box Stall Post.

8 ft. high.

Each........$31.00

FIG. 328 K

Stall Post.

For both box and open stalls.

Very Massive.

Generally used in connection with fixtures furnished by us to take the place of English fittings.

FIG. 329 K
Iron Stall Post Socket.
For 6 inch square Wood Post.
18 inches high, each..............$9.00

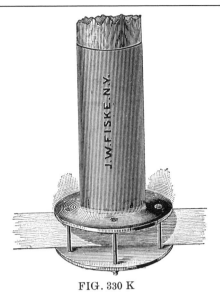

FIG. 330 K
Iron Stall Post Socket.
For 6 inch Wood Post, to bolt through
floor, with plate below.
8 inches high, each.. ....$3.50
15 "   "   " 4.00
Bolts Extra.

FIG. 331 K
Iron Socket.
For 6 inch Wood Post.
8 inches high, each... ....$2.25
15 "   "   " 3.00

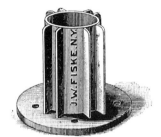

FIG. 332 K
Iron Stall Post Socket.
For 6 inch Wood Post, made to receive
Partitions from one to four sides.
15 inches high each.

1 Grove, each...... ....$4.50
2 Groves, " 5.50
3   "   " 6.50
4   "   " 7.50

FIG. 333 K
Iron Stall Post Socket.
For 6 inch Wood Post.
3¼ inches high, each..............$2.00
6   "   "   " 2.50
8   "   "   " 2.75

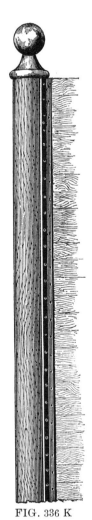

FIG. 336 K
Stall Partition Angle Iron.
For Wood Posts.
4 feet 6 inches high.
Per pair........................ $2.25

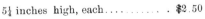

FIG. 334 K
Iron Stall Post Socket.
For 6 inch Wood Post.
5¼ inches high, each........... . $2.50

FIG. 335 K
Iron Stall Post Socket.
For 6 inch Square Wood Post.
8 inches high, each..............$3.00

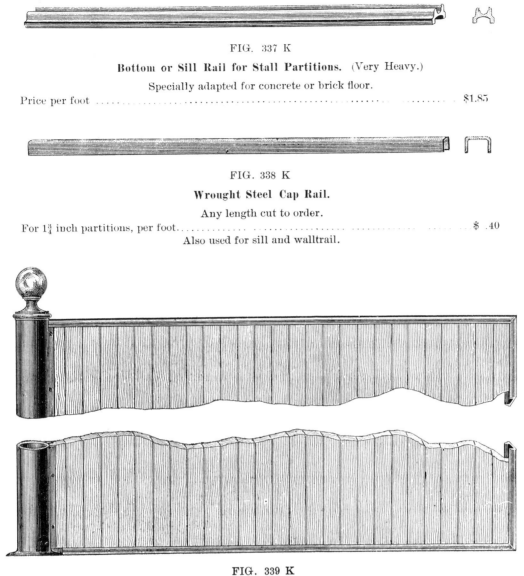

FIG. 337 K

Bottom or Sill Rail for Stall Partitions. (Very Heavy.)

Specially adapted for concrete or brick floor.

Price per foot $1.85

FIG. 338 K

Wrought Steel Cap Rail.

Any length cut to order.

For 1¾ inch partitions, per foot.................. .... $ .40

Also used for sill and walltrail.

FIG. 339 K

Showing Iron Stall Post with Cap, Sill and Wall Rail, fitted for Wood Partition.
For prices of Sill, Wall and Cap Rail. See Page 104.

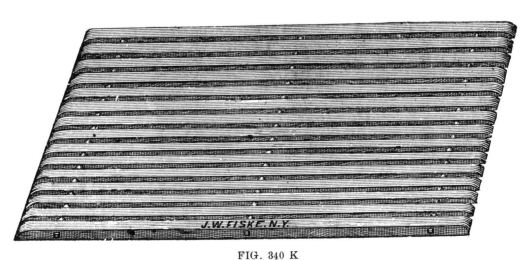

FIG. 340 K

Portable Wood Stall Flooring.

Price per square foot, including Iron Rods and Washers............................ $0.45
Iron Bolts, 2 feet 6 inches long, ½ inch diameter, each......................... .30
Cast Iron Washers, ½ inch thick, each... .02½
Any size made to order.

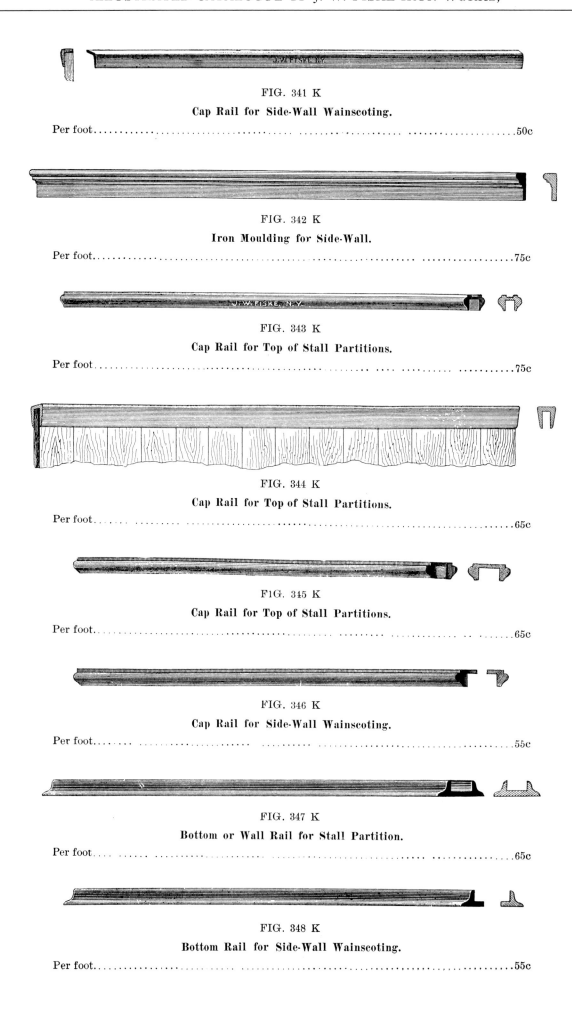

FIG. 341 K

Cap Rail for Side-Wall Wainscoting.

Per foot...50c

FIG. 342 K

Iron Moulding for Side-Wall.

Per foot...75c

FIG. 343 K

Cap Rail for Top of Stall Partitions.

Per foot...75c

FIG. 344 K

Cap Rail for Top of Stall Partitions.

Per foot...65c

FIG. 345 K

Cap Rail for Top of Stall Partitions.

Per foot...65c

FIG. 346 K

Cap Rail for Side-Wall Wainscoting.

Per foot...55c

FIG. 347 K

Bottom or Wall Rail for Stall Partition.

Per foot...65c

FIG. 348 K

Bottom Rail for Side-Wall Wainscoting.

Per foot...55c

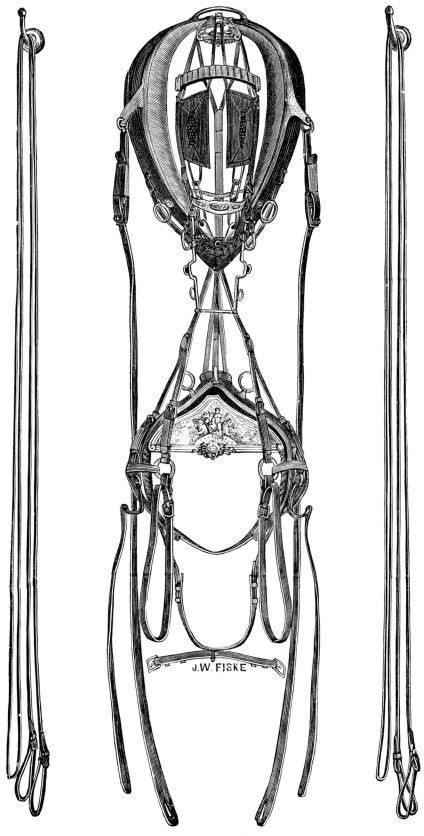

FIG. 349 K

French Set of Harness Brackets.

er Set, Iron, Bronzed Finish........................ ....$ 5.00
er Set, Brass or Bronze........................... .... 45.00

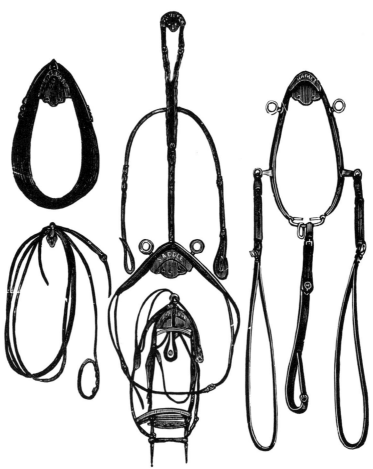

FIG. 350 K

Design representing an improved method of hanging up light Harness on Iron Brackets.

Separate Bracket for Each Piece of Harness.

Per Set.... ....$1.75

Method of Hanging Heavy Single and Double Harness in Sets on Ventilating Brackets, with
Polished Mahogany Finish or Ash Cappings.

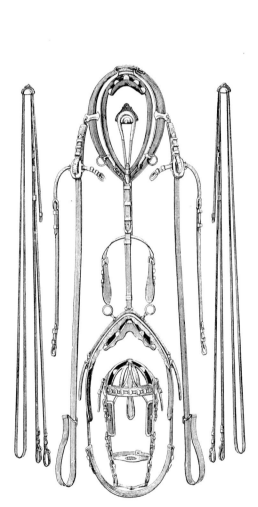

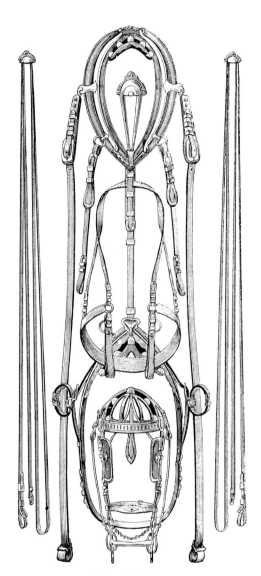

FIG. 351 K   FIG. 352 K

Single Harness Brackets.   **Double Harness Brackets.**

Per set, with polished wood cappings.................. ....$9.00   With polished wood cappings, per double set $18.00

☞See page 108 for illustration of brackets not mounted with harness.

Ventilating Harness Brackets with Polished Mahogany Finish or Ash Caps.

FIG. 353 K

Bridle Bracket.

For Light Harness.

Each $2.00

FIG. 354 K

Saddle Bracket.

For Light Harness.

Each...........................$2.25

FIG. 355 K

Dutch Collar Bracket.

For Light Harness.

Each.............................$2.00

Per Set, for Single Harness, including two Fig. 361 K, Rein Brackets and one Fig. 359 K, Crupper Bracket... .....$8.00

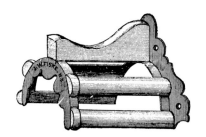

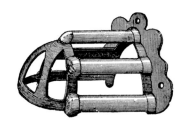

FIG. 356 K

Collar Bracket.

Each............................$2.75

Brass or Bronze,

Each $12.00

FIG. 357 K

Saddle Bracket.

Each............................$2.75

Brass or Bronze,

Each...........................$12.00

FIG. 358 K

Bridle Bracket.

Each.............................$2.50

Brass or Bronze,

Each...........................$12.00

FIG. 359 K

Crupper Bracket.

Each $0.75

Brass or Bronze,

Each $2.00

FIG. 360 K

Combination Collar and Bridle Bracket.

Each................................$4.00

Brass or Bronze, each................16.00

FIG. 361 K

Rein Bracket.

Each........ $0.50

Brass or Bronze,

Each........ $1.75

FIG. 362 K

Combination Bracket.

A complete set of Harness can be hung on this Bracket by hanging Collar and Bridle on upper part, allowing saddle to suspend by hanging Crupper on lower hook.

Each,.....,..............$3.75

Per Set for Single Harness, 5 pieces... $ 9.00

"   " Double "   10   " 18.00

☞See pages 107 and 109 for illustration of brackets in position with harness.

Method of Hanging Light Single and Double Harness on Ventilating Brackets with Polished
Mahogany Finish or Ash Cappings.

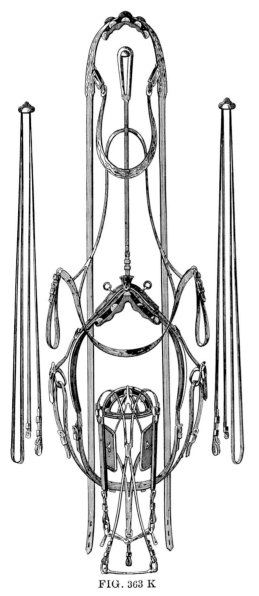

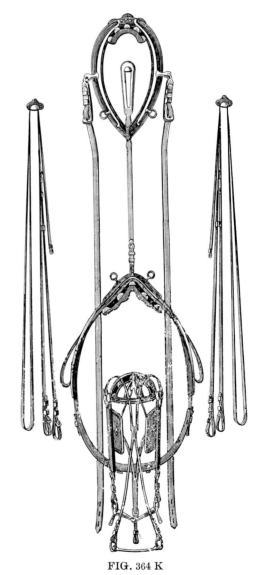

FIG. 363 K

Light Single Harness Brackets.

Per set, with polished wood cappings.......$8.00

FIG. 364 K

Light Double Harness Brackets.

Per set, with polished wood cappings.....$16.00

Ventilating Saddle and Bridle Brackets.

With Polished Mahogany Finish or Ash Cappings.

FIG. 365 K

Girth Hooks.

Hooks, Brass.

Per pair..................$2.00

FIG. 368 K

Stirrup Bracket.

Each...................$1.00

Brass or Bronze.

Each...................$3.00

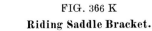

FIG. 366 K

Riding Saddle Bracket.

Each..$ 5.25

Brass or Bronze.

Each.......... .. .. 18.50

FIG. 367 K

Riding Bridle Bracket.

Each......... ....$1.25

Brass or Bronze.

Each.... ....$4.50

Method of Hanging Ladies' and Gents' Saddles and Bridles, Etc., on Ventilating Brackets,
with Polished Mahogany Finish or Ash Cappings.

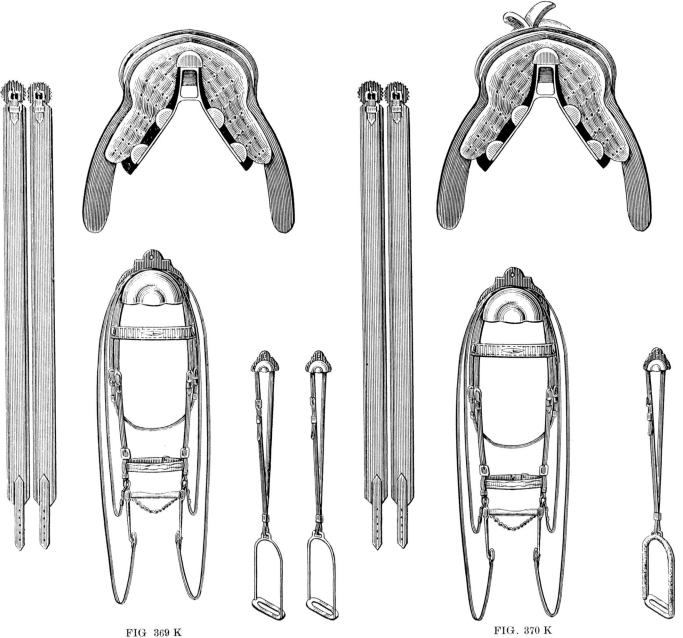

FIG 369 K

Per set, with polished wood cappings...................$8.00

FIG. 370 K

Per set, with polished wood cappings.............................$8.00

☞See above for illustration of brackets not mounted with saddles, etc.

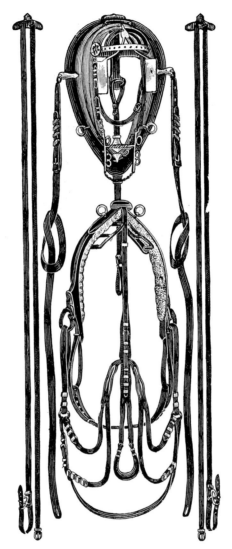

FIG. 371 K

Showing Single Harness Hung on Improved Iron Brackets.

Per Set, including one Bracket each, Figs. 375 K and 379 K, and two Rein Brackets as shown........$4.00

A complet Single Harness can be hung on Bracket Fig. 375 K, by hanging Collar and Bridle on upper
   part, allowing Saddle to suspend by hanging Crupper on lower hook, each. 1.80

For Double Harness it will require twice the number of Brackets.

FIG. 372 K

Collar and Bridle Bracket Combined.

Each...$1.80

A complete set of Harness can be hung on this Bracket by hanging Collar and Bridle on upper part, allowing saddle to suspend by hanging Crupper on lower hook.

FIG. 373 K

Rein Bracket.

Iron, Japanned, each....$0.50
Brass or Bronze, each.... 1.75

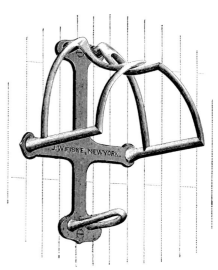

FIG. 374 K

Collar Bracket.

Each..........................$1.30

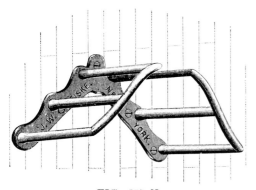

FIG. 375 K

Saddle Bracket.

Each..............................$1.55

FIG. 376 K

Dutch Collar Bracket.

Each $0.60

FIG. 377 K

Bracket for Holding a Complete Set of Harness.

Each................................$2.00

FIG. 378 K

Bridle Bracket.

Each.............................$1.55

FIG. 379 K

Harness Brackets.

Iron, Japanned, each....$2.00

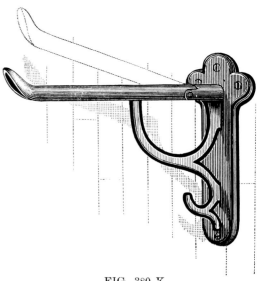

FIG. 380 K

Saddle Bracket.

With folding arm, particularly desirable where space is an object.

Each................................$2.25

Brackets for Set of Single Harness, Figs. 374 K, 375 K, 378 K, and two Rein Brackets, set. $5.30
Brackets for Double Harness, two of each, Figs. 374 K, 375 K, 378 K, and two Rein Brackets,.......... 9.70

New Design Ventilating Harness Brackets.

FIG. 381 K
Heavy Saddle Bracket.

Iron, Japanned, for single or double harness,
  each...................................$ 3.50
Brass or Bronze, each.... .... 12.00

FIG. 382 K
Light Saddle Bracket.

Iron, Japanned, for single or double harness,
  each.......................... ... .$ 3.00
Brass or Bronze, each....................... 10.00

FIG. 383 K
Collar Bracket.

Iron, Japanned, each.................... ....$1.50
Brass or Bronze, each 7.00

FIG. 384 K
Rein Bracket.

Iron, Japanned, each........................$1.50
Brass or Bronze, each........ .... 7.00

FIG. 385 K
Dutch Collar Bracket.

Iron, Japanned, each......... ....$2.25

FIG. 386 K
Crupper Bracket.
For light harness.

Iron, Japanned, each....$0.50
Brass or Bronze, each.... 1.75

FIG. 387 K
Bridle Bracket.

Iron, Japanned, each............$1.50
Brass or Bronze, each........... 7.00

FIG. 388 K
Crupper Bracket.
For heavy harness.

Iron, Japanned, each....$0.75
Brass, each............. 1.25

Brackets for heavy harness, Figs. 381 K 383 K, 384 K, 387 K, 388 K, per set, Iron, Japanned.....................$8.75
     "   " light   "   "   382 K, 383 K, 384 K, 386 K, 387 K,   "   "   " 8.00

FIG. 391 K

Harness Brackets.

Iron, Japanned, per set..............$4.00

FIG. 389 K

Ladies' Set.

Saddle, Bridle and Rein Brackets.

Iron, Japanned, per set......$ 4.00
Brass or Bronze, per set....... 22.00

FIG. 390 K

Gents' Set.

Saddle, Bridle and Rein Brackets.

Iron, Japanned, per set......$ 3.50
Brass or Bronze, per set..... . 20.00

FIG. 392 K

Bit Hook.

Brass, per dozen..............$1.50

FIG. 393 K

Bit Pin.

Brass, per dozen..............$1.50

FIG. 394 K

Hoof Cleaning Hook.

Brass, each...................$3.00
Iron, Japanned, each.......... .50

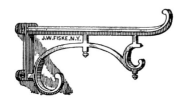

FIG. 395 K

Oiling and Washing Bracket.

Size, 10 inches.

Brass or Bronze, each........$4.50

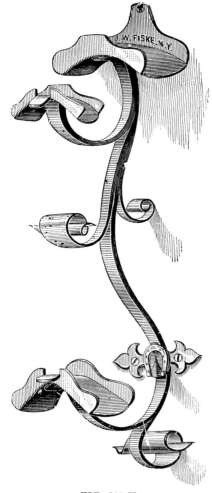

FIG. 397 K

Harness Bracket.

Holding a complete set of light harness.

Iron, Japanned, each....... ......$ 8.50
Brass or Bronze, each............. 40.00

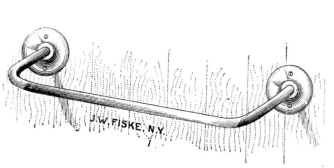

FIG. 396 K

Brass Chamois Rack.

No. 1.—1 foot 6 inches long, 3 inch projection, nickel plated, each........$2.00
No. 2.—2 feet 0   "   3 "   '.   "   " 2.65
No. 3.—2 feet 6   "   3 "   "   "   " 3.40

FIG. 398 K

Harness Hook.

Size, 8 inches.

Iron, Japanned.

Per doz..........$4.00

FIG. 399 K

Harness Hook.

Size, 8 inches.

Per doz., Iron, Jap'd..$4.00

" " Brass 48.00

FIG. 400 K

Wood Top Harness Bracket.

Each.............$1.00

FIG. 401 K

Harness Hook.

Size, 8 inches.

Iron, Japanned.

Per doz..........$2.00

FIG. 402 K

Harness Hook.

Size, 4½ inches, each	..$0.30
" 7 " "	.35
" 8 " "	.40
" 10 " "	.50

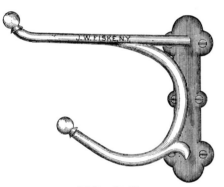

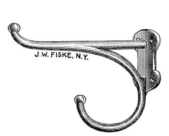

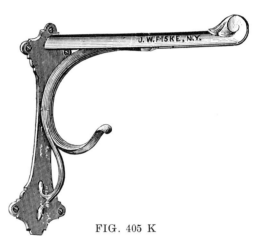

FIG. 403 K

Harness Hook.

Extra Heavy.

Upper Hook, 12 in., Lower Hook, 8½ in.

Per dozen.........................$16.50

FIG. 404 K

Harness Hook.—Extra Heavy.

No. 1. Size, 8 inches.
No. 2. " 10 "
No. 3. " 12 "

No. 1, per doz.. Jap'd........$ 4.00

" 2 " " " 9.00

" 3 " " " 10.00

FIG. 405 K

Ornamental Iron Harness Bracket.

Upper Hook, 14 in., Lower Hook, 6 in.

Each..................................$2.00

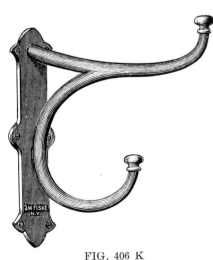

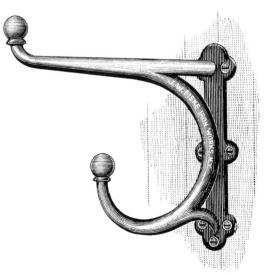

FIG. 406 K

Harness Hook.

Extra Heavy.

Iron, Japanned.

Upper Hook, 13 in., Lower Hook, 9 in.

Per dozen.........................$18.00

FIG. 407 K

Harness Hook.

Iron, Japanned.

Size, 6 in., per doz	......$1.50
" 8 " " "	.....2.50
" 10½ " " "	.....6.00
" 14 " " "	.....7.50
5 inches, Brass, each	...2.25
6 " " "	....2.75
8 " " "	....3.25

FIG. 408 K

Harness Hook.—Extra Heavy.

Iron, Japanned.

Upper Hook, 12 in., Lower Hook, 8 in.

Per dozen.........................$15.00

FIG. 409 K

Harness Bracket.

With Mahogany Finished Capping.

Each.................................$1.00

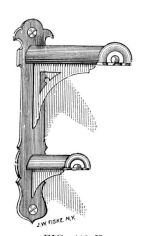

FIG. 410 K

Harness Bracket.

With Mahogany Finished Capping.

Each.................................$1.25

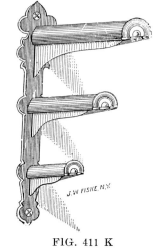

FIG. 411 K

Harness Bracket.

With Mahogany Finished Capping.

Each.................................$1.50

FIG. 412 K

Lantern Bracket.

Brass or Bronze, each $2.50
Lantern, Brass, each...........$1.50 to 5.00

FIG. 413 K

Blanket Bracket.

Without Wood Rollers.

Per pair...........................$1.25

FIG. 414 K

Lantern Bracket.

Each.................................80c

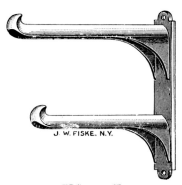

FIG. 415 K

Harness Bracket.

Size, Top Bracket, 8 in., Bottom
Bracket, 7 in.

Each...........................$1.25

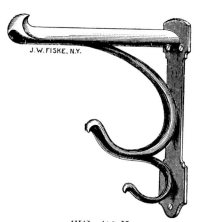

FIG. 416 K

Harness Bracket.

		Iron, Jap'd	Brass
Top Bracket, 10 inches, each......		$1.25	$8.00
" " 8 " "		1.00	7.00
" " 6 " "		.75	6.00

FIG. 417 K

**Bracket for Oiling and Washing
Harness.**

Each.................................80c

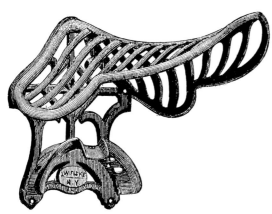

FIG. 418 K

Ladies' and Gents' Riding Saddle and Bridle Bracket.

Iron, Japanned, each.............................$ 7.00
Brass or Bronze, each........... .... 25.00

FIG. 419 K

Riding Sadle and Bridle Bracket.

No. 1.—Brass or Bronze, each........$25.00
No. 2.— " " " 16.00

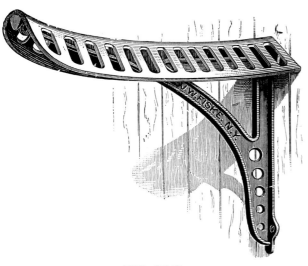

FIG. 420 K

Ladies' and Gents' Saddle Bracket.

For Ladies' Saddle, each.............................$2.75
For Gents' " " 2.50

FIG. 421 K

Ladies' and Gents' Saddle and Bridle Bracket.

For Ladies' Saddle, each............... ....$3.00
For Gents' " " 2.75

FIG. 422½ K

Gents' Riding Saddle Bracket.

Size, 20 inches x 16 inches, bronzed, each..............$4.00

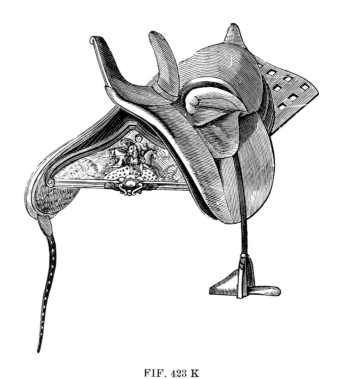

FIF. 423 K

Ladies' Riding Saddle Bracket.

Size, 27 inches x 16 inches, bronzed, each... ....$4.50

FIG. 424 K

Gents' Riding Saddle and Bridle Bracket.

Each.................................$1.50

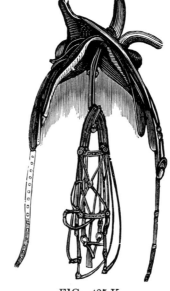

FIG. 425 K

Ladies' Riding Saddle and Bridle Bracket.

Each................. ....$1.75

FIG. 426 K

Riding Saddle and Bridle Bracket.

Each... ....$2.00

FIG. 427 K
Riding Bridle Bracket.
Each......................85c

FIG. 428 K
Riding Bridle Bracket.
Each......................85c

FIG. 429 K
Riding Bridle Bracket.
Each... ....85c

FIG. 430 K
Riding Bridle Bracket.
Each.... ....85c

FIG. 431 K
Riding Bridle Bracket.
Each...... ....85c

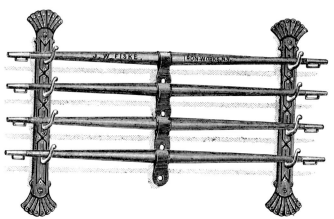

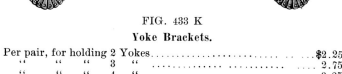

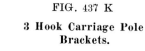

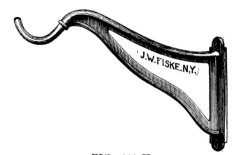

FIG. 432 K

Shaft or Coach Pole Bracket.

Covered with Rubber.

Per pair................$1.70

FIG. 433 K

Yoke Brackets.

Per pair, for holding 2 Yokes...........................$2.25
      "   "   "   3   " 2.75
      "   "   "   4   " 3.25

FIG. 434 K

Yoke Brackets.

Per pair, 4 hooks........$2.50
      "   "   3   " 2.00
      "   "   2   " 1.30
      "   "   1   "   .... .75

FIG. 438 K

Collar or Pole Bracket.

Each........................60c

FIG. 435 K

Pole Bracket.

1 Hook, Brass or Bronze, per pair.......$ 8.00
2 Hooks,   "   "   "   16.00
3   "   "   "   "   24.00
      "   "   "   "   32.00

FIG. 436 K

4 Hook Carriage Pole Brackets.

Per pair.................$3.00

FIG. 437 K

3 Hook Carriage Pole Brackets.

Per pair $2.50

FIG. 439 K

2 Hook Carriage Pole Brackets.

Per pair.................$1.50

FIG. 440 K   Single Hook Pole Brackets.

Per pair...$1.25

FIG. 441 K

Carriage Pole Bracket.

Jap., Iron, each...............$1.25
Polished, Brass or Bronze, each 5.25

FIG. 442 K

Yoke Bracket.

Each................20c

FIG. 443 K   Shaft Brackets.

Per Pair...$1.25

FIG. 444 K

Carriage Pole or Shaft Bracket.

Ends covered with rubber.

9 inches projection, per pair.......$2.25
12½   "   "   "   " 2.50
16   "   "   "   " 2.75

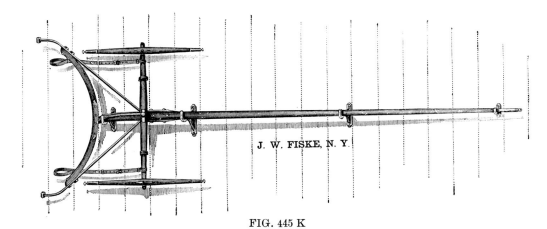

FIG. 445 K

Showing light carriage pole hung on a set of brackets of different lengths.

Per set, covered with rubber...$4.00

FIG. 446 K

Showing shafts of wagon hung on Fig. 444 K Shaft Brackets.

Per pair, covered with rubber...$2.60

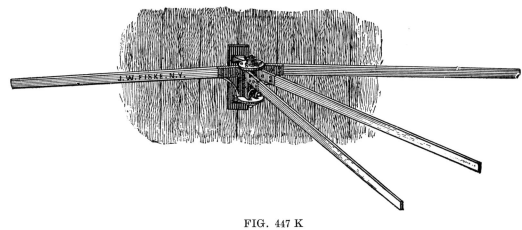

FIG. 447 K

Blanket Bracket with Black Walnut Arms.

Each $20.00

FIG. 448 K

Stationary Blanket Brackets.

For 3 rollers, per pair, without wood rollers $2.75
1¼ inch polished wood rollers, per foot 30

FIG. 449 K

Stationary Blanket Brackets.

Per pair, without wood rollers $2.25
1¾ inch polished wood roller, per foot 45

FIG. 450 K

Stationary Blanket Brackets.

Per set of 3 Brackets, without wood roller $4.00
2 inch polished wood roller, per foot 50

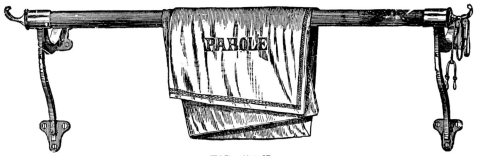

FIG. 451 K

Stationary Blanket Brackets.

Iron, Japanned, per pair, without wood roller...$ 3.50
1¼ inch polished wood roller, per foot... .... .30
Brass, per pair, without wood roller... 18.00

FIG. 452 K

Swinging Blanket Brackets.

Iron, Japanned, per pair, without wood roller.... ....$ 6.00
1⅝ inch polished wood roller, per foot............................ .... .45
Brass, per pair, without wood roller................ .... 40.00

FIG. 453 K

Swinging Blanket Brackets.

Iron, Japanned, per pair, without wood roller.... ....$ 5.00
2¾ inch polished wood roller, per foot... .60
Brass, per pair, without wood roller.. 28.00

FIG. 454 K

Stationary Blanket Brackets.

Iron, Japanned, per pair, without wood roller......................................$ 3.50
2¾ inch polished wood roller, per foot... .60
Brass per pair, without wood roller.. 25.00

FIG. 455 K

Blanket Brackets.

Per pair, without wood roller...$4.00
3½ inch polished wood roller, per foot.. .75

FIG. 456 K

Blanket Brackets.

Per pair, without wood roller..$1.25
1½ inch polished wood roller, per foot... .35

FIG. 457 K

Swinging Blanket Brackets.

Per pair, without wood roller $3.00
2 inch polished wood roller, per foot... .50

FIG. 458 K

Swinging Blanket Brackets.

Per pair, without wood roller...$3.00

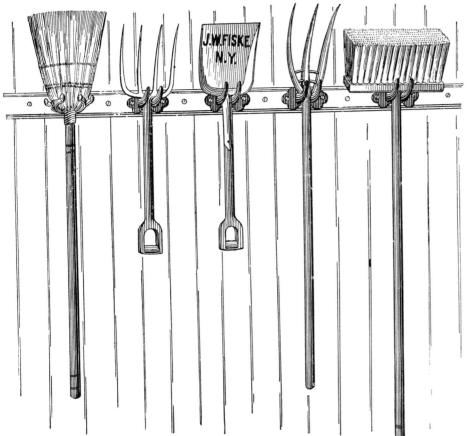

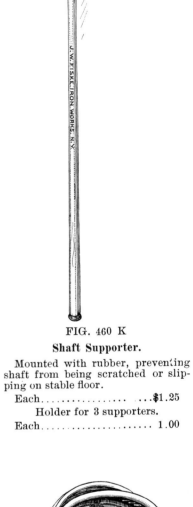

FIG. 459 K

Implement Holder.

A very convenient article in the stable, each.....................................$ .35
Stable Brooms, each... 1.00
Rattan Brooms, each.. 1.00
Shovels, each.. 1.50
Steel Hay Forks, each.. 1.00

FIG. 460 K

Shaft Supporter.

Mounted with rubber, preventing shaft from being scratched or slipping on stable floor.
Each...................$1.25
Holder for 3 supporters.
Each........................ 1.00

FIG. 461 K

Broom Holder.

Iron, Japanned, each.................$0.40
Brass or Bronze, each 3.00

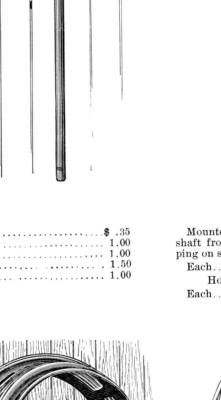

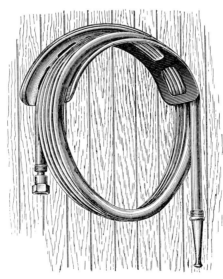

FIG. 462 K

Steel Wheelbarrow.

Capacity, 3 cubic feet of earth.

Each ....$9.00 to $13.00

Other sizes furnished.

FIG. 463 K

Hose Bracket

Two Sizes.

No. 1. 5½ inches projection, each......$3.00
No. 2. 8 "   "   " 4.50

FIG. 464 K

Hose Bracket.

Ordinary Size.

Iron, Japanned, each......$2.25
Brass or Bronze, each...... 7.00

FIG. 465 K

Implement Holder.

Showing Broom hung in position.

FIG. 466 K

Fork Holder.

Showing Fork hung in position.

FIG. 467 K

Broom Jacket and Cap.

Showing same in position.

FIG. 468 K

Shovel Holder.

Showing Shovel hung in position

FIG. 469 K

Implement Holder.

Brass, heavy, each....$4.00
" light, " 3.00

FIG. 470 K

Fork Holder.

Brass, each.........$4.00

FIG. 472 K

Broom Hook.

Brass or Bronze, each....$3.00

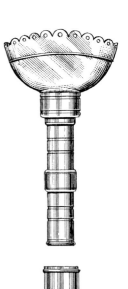

FIG. 474 K

Broom Jacket and Cap.

	Each
Jacket, brass...	$4.75
Cap, Brass....	.75

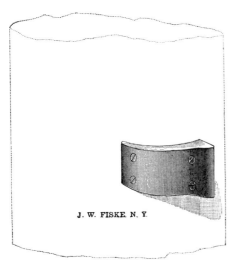

J. W. FISKE. N. Y.

FIG. 471 K

Box Stall Door Stop.

Brass or Bronze, each................. ....80c

FIG. 473 K

Shovel Holder.

Brass or Bronze, each....$3.50

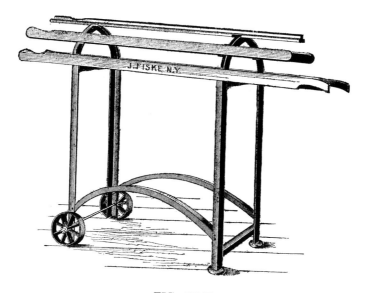

FIG. 475 K

Movable Wrought Iron Harness Cleaning Horse.

With wood cappings, each..$15.00

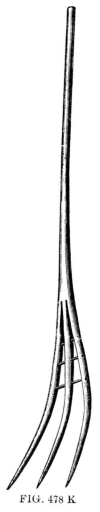

FIG. 476 K

Stall Hook.

Each.............$1.00

FIG. 477 K

Movable Wooden Harness Horse with Hooks.

For holding Harness and Drawers which slide both ways.

In Varnished White Pine, each.................................$45.00

FIG. 478 K

Wooden Stable Fork.

Each.............$1.50

FIG. 479 K.

Ornamental Iron Pail Stand.

For one pail, 17 inches long...$20.00
For two pails, 31 inches long 30.00
For three pails, 46 inches long..... .... 45.00
Oak pail, with solid bronze hoops, handle and monograms, to order..... .... 30.00
Oak pail, with brass trimmings and monograms, to order.. . 25.00
Oak pail, with galvanized iron hoops and handles.. 2.00

FIG. 480 K

Harness Cleaning Horse with Table and Drawers.

The leaves fold up against centre standards, when not in use.

In Varnished Oak, each...$100.00

FIG. 481 K

Ash Girth Drier.

To take 4 girths, each.............$12.00
"   6   "   " 14.00
"   8   "   " 16.00

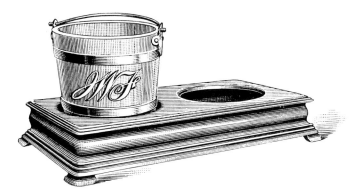

FIG. 482 K

Wood Pail Holder.

For two, three or four Pails.

In varnished oak, for 2 pails, each........................$25.00
"   "   "   " 3 "   " 35.00
"   "   "   " 4 "   " 40.00

Oak Pails with solid cast brass or bronze mountings, initials or
    monogram, each..................................$30.00
Oak Pails, with brass mountings, letters or monograms, each $20.00

FIG. 483 K

Polished Steel Pillar Chain.

Each...... ....$4.00

FIG. 484 K

Pillar Cord.

With Brass Snaps, per pair.......................... ......$6.00

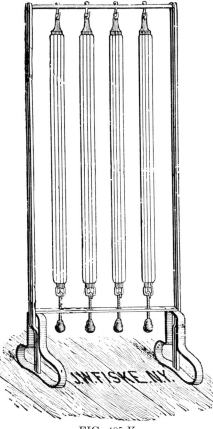

FIG. 485 K

Wrought Iron Saddle Girth Drier.

To take 4 girths, each...............$ 7.00
"   6 "   " 10.00
"   8 "   " 12.00

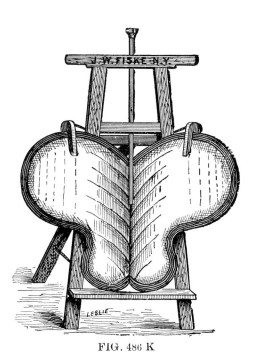

FIG. 486 K

Saddle Airer.

For holding the saddle and exposing the
damp surface of the pads to the drying influ-
ence of the fire or sun.

In selected white pine, varnished each...$7.00

FIG. 487 K

Kicking Mat

For sides of stalls, any size made to order
plain, or with border and monogram, including Brass fixtures for securing mats to
sides of stall. Any size

Prices on application.

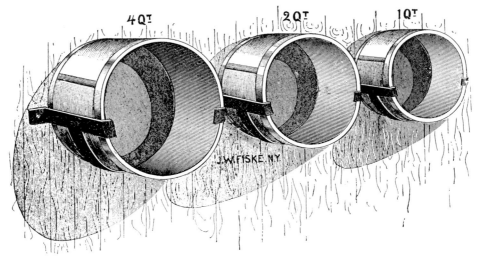

FIG. 488 K

Grain Measure Holders.

Holder for 1 quart measure, each... ....$0.50
    "   " 2   "   "   " .... .65
    "   " 4   "   "   " 1.00

FIG. 489 K

Wrought Iron Oiling and Washing Bracket.

Each.................$3.50

If covered with leather, add to above prices, $3.50

FIG. 490 K

Wrought Iron Oiling and Washing Bracket.

Each.................$4.00

FIG. 491 K

Iron Telescopic Oiling and Washing Bracket.

Which can be raised and lowered at will.

Each.................$5.50

FIG. 492 K

Oiling and Washing Bracket with best Leather Strap.

Each........... ....$3.00

Brass Hook and Russet Leather Strap, each, 9.00

If covered with leather, add to above prices, $2.00

FIG. 493 K

Wrought Iron Telescopic Oiling and Washing Bracket.

which can be raised and lowered at will.

Each........................$9.00

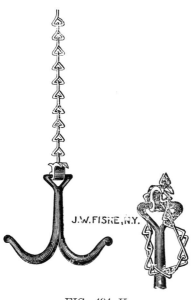

FIG. 494 K

Oiling and Washing Bracket.

With Grip Chain, which allows the hook to be raised or lowered at will.

Each.................... .....$1.50

FIG. 495 K

Wrought Iron Oiling and Washing Bracket.

Each..........................$4.00

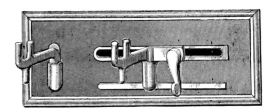

FIG. 496 K

Bit Cleaner.

With polished moving parts.

Each.......... ....$6.50

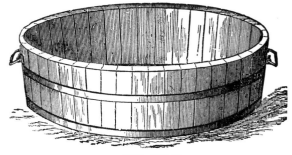

FIG. 497 K

Soaking Tub.

23 inches long, 17 inches wide. Galvanized Trimmings.

Each..$6.00

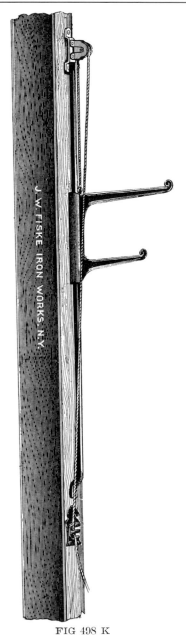

FIG 498 K

Adjustable Sliding Harness Hook.

Arranged with pulley, rope and cleat specially adapted for stables where it is desirable to hang harness on posts at rear of stalls, and can be raised and lowered at will.

Upper Hook, 11½ in. Lower Hook, 6 in. projection.

Complete, Japanned, each............$3.50

FIG. 499 K

Stable Stove with Copper Boiler and N. P. Faucet.

12 inch stove	$14.00	Boiler for 12 inch stove, 4 gals.	$11.00
14 " "	19.00	" 14 " " 7 "	12.00
16 " "	22.00	" 16 " " 10 "	14.00

FIG. 500 K

Iron Box for Holding Stopping Mixture.

Each...................................$2.25

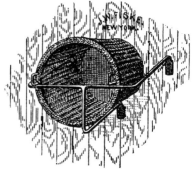

FIG. 501 K

Wrought Iron Basket Holder.

Each............................$1.75

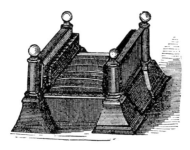

FIG. 502 K

Brush Foot Scraper.

Each...........................$3.00
Extra brushes, each, net........   .52

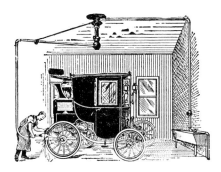

FIG. 503 K

The "Utility" Washing Device.

Adapted for automobile carriages, cars, wagons, trucks, etc.

Each $45.00

FIG. 504 K

The "Elite" Washing Device.

Particularly adapted for private stables.

Each $54.00

FIG. 505 K

The "Leader" Washing Device.

Plain, Simple and Strong.

Each $30.00

FIG. 506 K

The "Favorite" Washing Device.

Particularly adapted for Livery, Boarding and Business Stables, and will stand hard useage. Is simple in construction, strong and durable.

Each $38.00

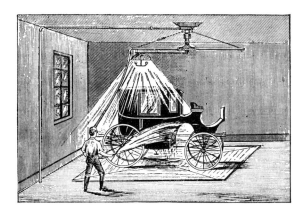

Patented May 2, 1899.

FIG. 507 K

The "Superior" Washing Device.

This is the only Illuminated Washer on the market, and is fully protected by patents. Allows the washing of carriages at night or in dark places, throwing the light where it is needed.

No. 1, for Gas.   No. 2, for Electricity.

Each $60.00

Patented May 2, 1899,

FIG. 508 K

The "Excelsior" Washing Device.

This Device is specially recommended on account of its construction. The braces are strong and will keep the machine in line and joint working freely.

Each $23.00

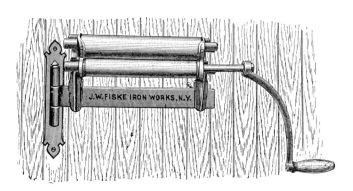

FIG. 509 K

Chamois or Towel Wringer.

Mounted on Iron Swinging Bracket.

Each, including Wringer and Bracket....................$6.00

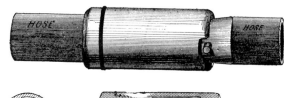
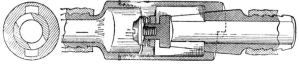

Patented May 2, 1899.

FIG. 510 K

The "Simplicity" Water Cut Off.

Made all of brass, and for ¾ inch hose. Neat, simple and strong, and by a slight turn of the Device the water is turned on or off. It is convenient for masons' use in mixing water, for lawn hose and for any place where hose is used and water is liable to be left running. Will soon pay for itself.

Each.................................. ....$4.00

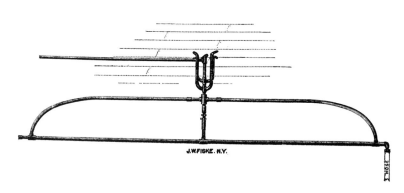

FIG. 511 K

Carriage Washing Device.

Simpson's Patent.

Is well regarded and guaranteed as represented. Is made of the best material. No stable keeper can afford to be without a washing device, and are equally necessary for private use, being economical, saving both hose and time.

Each............................... ....$22.00

FIG. 512 K

Carriage or Automobile Washing Device.

Each........... ....$16.00

FIG. 513 K

Carriage Brush.

With Coupling for Rubber Hose.

Particularly adapted for washing carriages, the Brush being soft and at the same time supplied with water.

Each.. ....$6.50

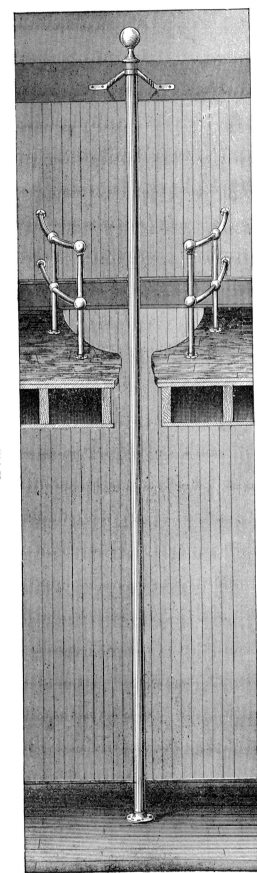

FIG. 514 K

Brass Sliding Pole and Guard Rails for Fire Engine House.

Pole Polished Brass Rail, 2 inch diameter including flange at bottom and ball top finish, with braces of iron, per foot..$ 2.50

Guard Rails, 3 feet long each, 1½ inch diameter, brass, per pair........................ 60.00

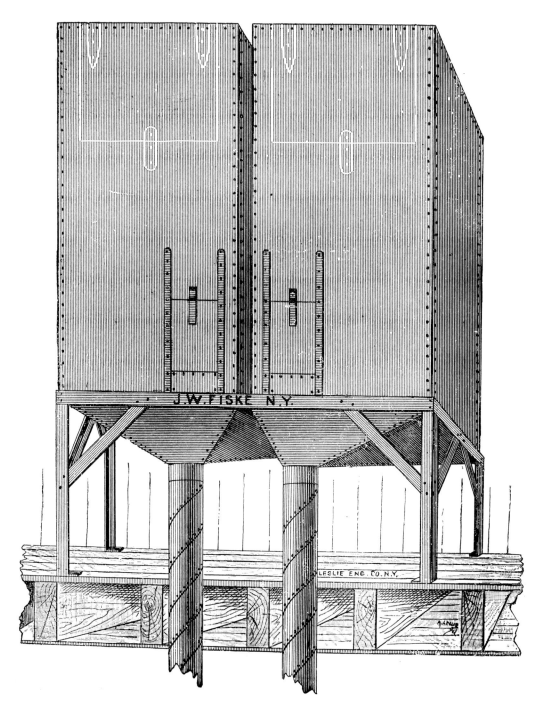

FIG. 515 K

Galvanized Iron Feed Bin.

Any size made to order.   Prices given upon application.

☞This Feed Bin has been adopted by the N. Y. Fire Department, and has been put in many stables in New York and other cities for which we have furnished Stable Fixtures.

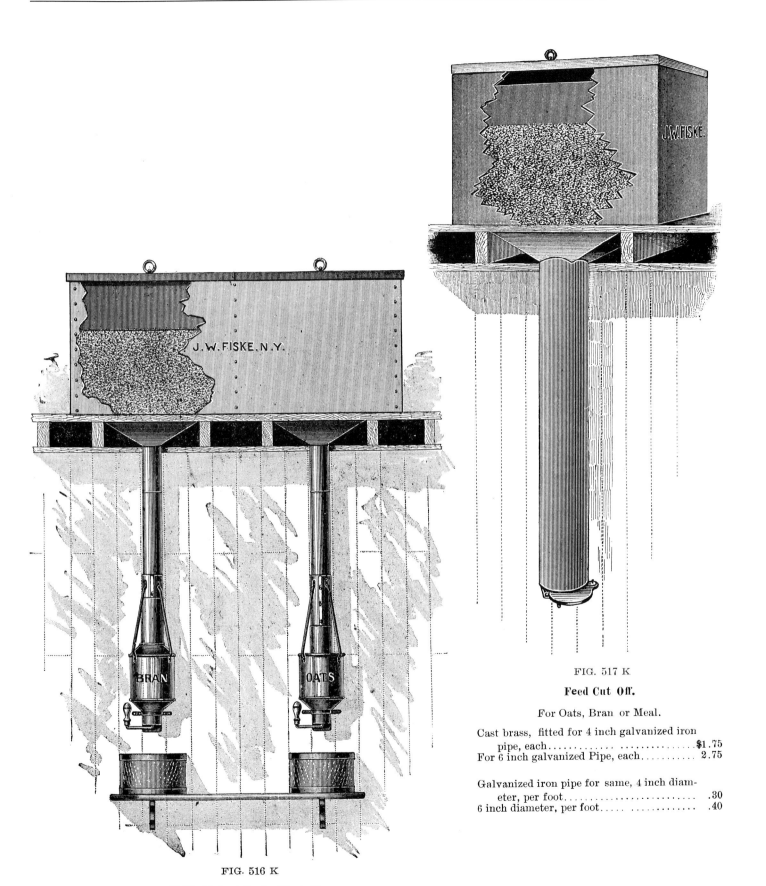

FIG. 517 K

Feed Cut Off.

For Oats, Bran or Meal.

Cast brass, fitted for 4 inch galvanized iron
  pipe, each............... ....$1.75
For 6 inch galvanized Pipe, each.......... 2.75

Galvanized iron pipe for same, 4 inch diameter, per foot......................... .30
6 inch diameter, per foot.... .... .40

FIG. 516 K

Bell's Patent Grain Measure.

By raising or lowering the inside cone, the capacity of grain measure can
be increased or diminished, and from three to six quarts discharged. Being
of galvanized iron are far more desirable than the old style wood chute.

Measure only for Oats, each.$6.50 For Bran, which does not measure, each $5.00
Galvanized Iron Pipe for same, 4 in. diameter, per foot.................... 30c.

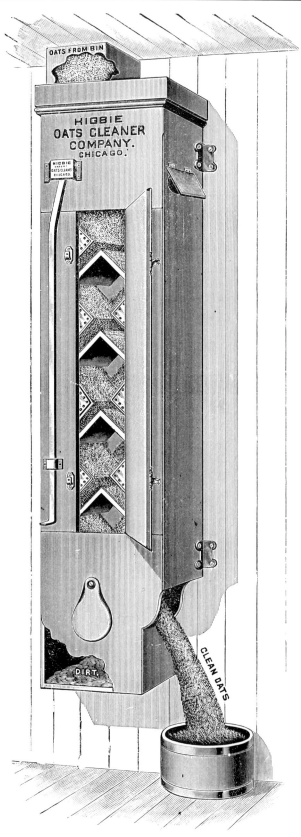

FIG. 518 K

Oat Cleaner.

(Higbie's Patent.)

No. 1.—6 feet 3 inches long, 9 x 14 inches. Capacity, ½ bushel per minute.........$25.00
"   2.—6 "   3   "   "   11 x 14   "   "   1   "   "   " 27.50
"   3.—6 "   3   "   "   13 x 14   "   "   2 bushels "   " 30.00
"   4.—8 "   6   "   "   15 x 24   "   "   4   "   "   " 40.00

Special sizes made to order, price depending upon the size. Cleaners can also be made to order from any kind of wood and trimmed with iron, brass or bronze as desired, at an additional cost.

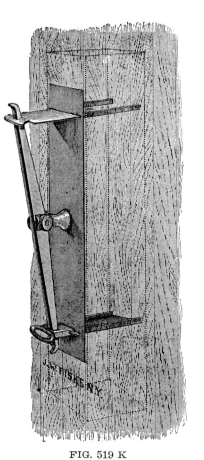

FIG. 519 K

Feed Cut Off.

Which governs the supply of feed from the Bin in the loft to the stable below, the capacity between the blades being 4 quarts, and enables the attendant to feed his stock with a correct knowledge of quantity used.

Galvanized iron, each..........$8.00

Galvanized iron with Brass
    Handles and Bearings, each. 10.00

FIG. 520 K

Feed cut off for oats, bran or meal.

Jap'd   Galv.
For 4 in. gal pipe.....$1.75 $2.25
" 6   "   " 2.25   3.00

FIG. 521 K

Name Plate.

Each, bronzed............$1.00

FIG. 522 K

Name Plate.

Diameter, 11⅝ inches.

Iron, bronzed, each................$3.00
Iron, with brass tie ring, each........ 5.50

FIG. 523 K

Name Plate.

Each, bronzed............$1.00

FIG. 524 K

Interchangeable Name Plate.

Not including painting of Name, bronzed, each........ ....$1.50
Brass or Bronze, each.................... .... 7.00

FIG. 525 K

Name Plate.

Each, bronzed............$1.00

FIG. 526 K

Interchangeable Name Plate.

Not including name, bronzed, each......... ....$4.00

FIG. 527 K

Name Plate.

To hold card with name of horse.

No. 1. Each.... ....50c
No. 2. " 25c

FIG. 528 K

Tie Ring and Name Plate.

Brass, each.......... ... ...$10.00

FIG. 529 K

Tie Ring and Name Plate.

Brass, each....... .. ....$10.00

FIG. 530 K

Tie Ring and Name Plate.

Brass, each......... ......$10.00

FIG. 531 K

Hitching Bar.

Allowing the horse more freedom in stall when tied.

Each..................$1.80

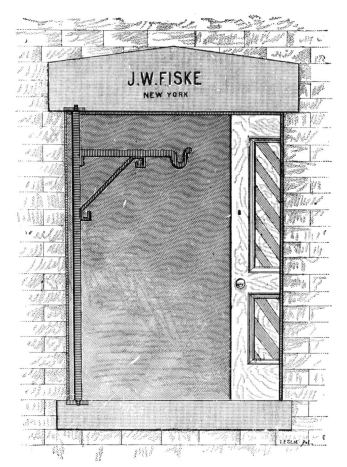

J.W. FISKE
NEW YORK

FIG. 532 K

Movable Wrought Iron Crane.

For Hoisting Hay, Grain, etc.

Each, depending on size and weight to hoist, from..$12.00 to $20.00

FIG. 533 K

Tie Ring for Round Post.

Each, plain................$0.75
  "   bronzed............. 1.00

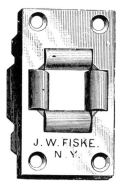

FIG. 534 K

Halter Sheave with Rollers.

Size 4½ x 2½ inches, each...75c

J.W. FISKE
N.Y.

FIG. 535 K

Halter Sheave with Rollers.

Each..................$1.50

J.W. FISKE. N.Y.

FIG. 536 K

Horse Weight.

No. 1. Japanned, each.....$1.50
  " 2.   "   " 2.00
  " 3.   "   " 2.25

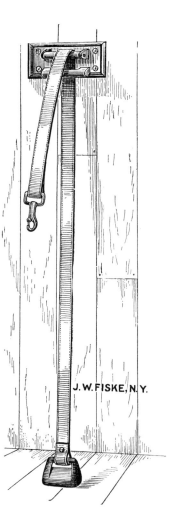

J.W. FISKE, N.Y.

FIG. 538 K

Tie Strap.

With Roller Plate and Weight.

Each $3.00

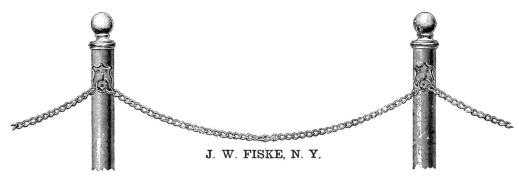

J. W. FISKE, N. Y.

FIG. 537 K

Chain Snaps and Post Rings.

Single chain, including snap, 3 feet long...$1.25   Double chain, including snap, 6 feet long...$2.50
Post Rings, each.... .. ..50c

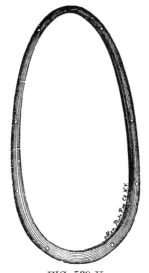

FIG. 539 K

Iron Collar or Frame.

For opening of Manger at head of stalls when boarded up in front, as in old-fashioned stables, through which the horse eats, and prevents him nibbling the woodwork.

Each.........................$2.25

FIG. 540 K

Anchor Tie Ring.

Each, plain............50c
" galvanized........65c

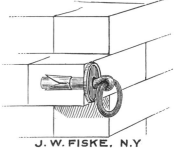

J. W. FISKE. N.Y
FIG. 541 K

Expansion Bolt Tie Ring.

Each, plain.................$1.00

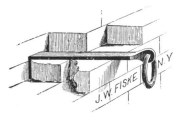

FIG. 542 K

Anchor Tie Ring.

Each.....................50c

FIG. 543 K

Anchor Sliding Tie Bar.

Each, plain...........$1.75
" galvanized.......2.50

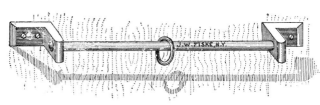

FIG. 544 K

Hitching Bar.

Allowing the horse more freedom in stall when tied.
Each......................................$1.75

FIG. 545 K

Stair Plate, with or Without Nosing.

19 inches x 5 inches with nosing, $.60 each, without nosing, $0.55
22	"	x 6	"	"	"	.70 "	"	"	.65
30	"	x 6	"	"	"	1.25 "	"	"	1.20
36	"	x 6	"	"	"	1.45 "	"	"	1.35
36	"	x 8	"	"	"	1.65 "	"	"	1.55
42	"	x 9	"	"	"	2.35 "	"	"	2.25

Any size made to order.   Estimates given upon application.

FIG. 547 K

Nibbling Roller.

Each, including sockets, 4 feet 6 inches long................$4.00
Any length made to order.

Front View. Back View.

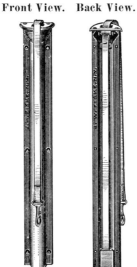

FIG. 546 K

Hitching Arrangement.

Each....................$5.00

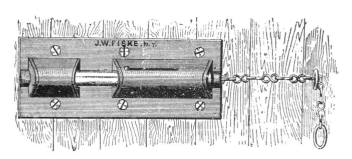

FIG. 548 K

Hitching Bolt.

Each, Japanned...$2.50

FIG. 549 K

Horse Head for Wood Post.

Each, painted........$3.00
"   bronzed......... 3.75

FIG. 550 K

Overhead Hitching Attachments.

For single or double team.   Very convenient for hitching horses on carriage house floor.

Price, complete, including rope, cleat, pulleys and snap......$2.50

FIG. 551 K

Post Cap for Wood Post.

For 6 in. diameter Post.

Each................$1.50

FIG. 552 K

Plain Cap for Wood Post.

No. 1. Each, japan'd for 4 in. post.$1.25
No. 2. Each, japan'd for 5 in. post. 1.50

FIG. 553 K

Post Cap.

For 4 inch diameter post, each......50c

FIG. 554 K

Pineapple Head for Post.

Each, painted............$3.00
"   bronzed... .... 3.50

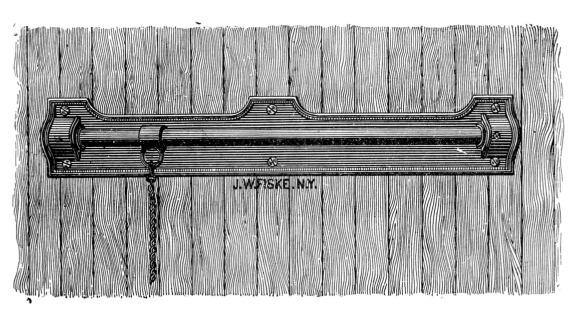

FIG. 555 K

Recessed Sliding Hitching Bar.

For fastening up Horse in Box Stalls, allowing him to move from side to side.

With brass runner and polished iron sliding bar, each..$10.00

FIG. 556 K

Horse Shoe Tie Ring.

Each, plain..........40c
"   galvanized.....60c

FIG. 557 K

Plain Tie Ring.

Each, plain..........40c
"   galvanized.....60c

FIG. 558 K

Double Ring.
For Post at foot of stall to prevent horses from backing out.
Each..............60c

FIG. 559 K

Tie Ring.

Each, plain..........40c
"   galvanized.....60c

FIG. 560 K

Tie Ring.

Each, plain..........60c
"   galvonized.....75c

FIG. 561 K

Lion Head Tie Ring.

Each, plain.......$0.75
"   galvanized... 1.00

FIG. 562 K

Dog Head Tie Ring.

Each, plain.......$1.50
"   galvanized .. 2.00

FIG. 563 K

Lion Head Tie Ring.

Each, plain.......$0.75
"   galvanized... 1.00

FIG. 564 K

Horse Head Tie Ring.

Each, plain.......$1.50
"   galvanized... 2.00

FIG. 565 K

Ornamental Tie Ring.

Each, plain.........50c
"   galvanijed.....65c

FIG. 566 K

Ornamental Tie Ring.

Each, plain...... .50c
"   galvanized.....65c

FIG. 567 K

Ornamental Tie Ring.

Each, plain........50c
"   galvanized.....65c

FIG. 568 K

Ornamental Tie Ring.

Each, plain.........50c
"   galvanized.....65c

FIG. 569 K

Shield Tie Ring.

Each, plain.........40c
"   galvanized ...60c

FIG. 570 K

Diamond Tie Ring.

Each, plain.........40c
"   galvanized.....60c

FIG. 571 K

Ram's Head Tie Ring.

Each, plain $1.75
"   galvanized.. 2.00

FIG. 572 K

Tie Ring.

Each, plain.........40c
"   galvanized.....60c

FIG. 573 K

Tie Ring.

Each, plain.........40c
"   galvanized.....50c

FIG. 574 K

Tie Ring.

Each, plain.........40c
"   galvanized.....60c

FIG. 575 K

Tie Ring.

Each, plain.........40c
"   galvanized.....60c

FIG. 576 K

Tie Ring.

Each, plain. 35c
"   galvanized.....50c

FIG. 577 K

Tie Ring.

Each, plain.........35c
"   galvanized.....50c

FIG. 578 K

Lion Head Tie Ring.

Brass, each $6.00

FIG. 579 K

Tie Ring.

Brass, each.......$4.00

FIG. 580 K

Tie Ring.

Brass, each........$3.00

FIG. 581 K

Lion Head Tie Ring.

Brass, each.......$6.00

FIG. 582 K

Tie Ring.
(Very Heavy.)

Brass, each.......$5.00

FIG. 583 K

Tie Ring.
(Very Heavy.)

Brass, each.......$4.50

FIG. 584 K

Tie Ring.

2 Sizes.

Brass, each.......$2.00
"   " 1.50

FIG. 585 K

Bit Tie Ring.

Brass, each......... ....$5.50

FIG. 586 K

Horse Shoe Tie Ring.

2 Sizes.

Brass, each.......$5.00
"   " 7.00

FIG. 587 K

Tie Ring.

Brass, each...... .$3.00

FIG. 588 K

Tie Ring.

Brass, each.......$4.00

FIG. 589 K

Tie Ring.

Brass, each.......$3.00

FIG. 590 K

Lion Head Tie Ring.

2 sizes.

Brass, each..... .. $6.00
"   " 9.00

FIG. 591 K

Tie Ring.

Brass, each.......$3.50

FIG. 592 K

Tie Ring.

Brass, each.......$3.25

FIG. 593 K

Tie Ring.

Brass, each..... ..$2.75

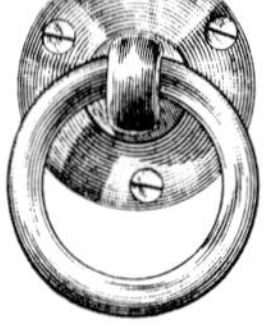

FIG. 594 K

Tie Ring.

Brass, each.......$3.00

FIG. 595 K

Tie Ring.

Brass, each.......$3.00

FIG. 596 K

Tie Ring.
(Extra Heavy.)

Brass, each $5.00

☞The above Tie Rings are made of either Brass or Bronze.

FIG. 597 K

Brass Post Caps.

For 2⅝ inch diameter
Post.
Each $13.00

For 5 inch diameter
Post.
Each. $20.00
" cast iron. 4.00

For 6 inch diameter
Post.
Each $20.00
" cast iron. 5.00

FIG. 598 K

Brass Post Cap

For 3½ inch diameter
Post.
Each. $15.00

FIG. 599 K

Brass Post Cap.
With Side Rings.
For 4½ inch diameter Post.
Each. $7.50
For 6 inch diameter Post.
Each. $10.00

FIG. 600 K

Brass Post Cap.
Very Heavy.

For 5 inch diameter
Post.
Each. $25.00

FIG. 601 K

Brass Post Cap.

For 6 inch diameter
Post.
Each. $27.00

FIG. 602 K

Sponge and Wet Brush Racks.
Two Sizes.

No. 1. Size, 14 in. long, 6¼ in. wide.
Each. $1.50
No. 2. Size, 23 in. long, 7¼ in. wide.
Each. $3.00

FIG. 603 K

Match Box.

Brass, each. $4.50

FIG. 604 K

Sponge Rack.

Brass, 14 inch, each. $27.00
"   22   "   " 39.00

FIG. 605 K
**Wrought Iron Corner
Salt Dish.**
Each. $1.75

FIG. 606 K

Sponge and Wet Brush Rack.
Each $1.25

FIG. 607 K

**Salt Dish or Dry Brush
Box.**
Each. 80c

FIG. 608 K

Corner Salt Dish
Each. 75c

J. W. FISKE. N.Y.

FIG. 609 K

Soap Dish.

Brass, each $3.50

J. W. FISKE, N.Y.

FIG. 610 K

Tumbler Holder.

Brass, each $3.50

FIG. 611 K

Soap Dish.

Brass, each $6.50

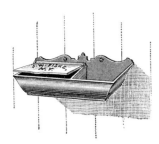

FIG. 612 K

Match Box with Cover.

Double, to hold Burnt Matches.

Each .... .75c

FIG. 613 K

Soap Dish.

Each........................ 75c

J. W. FISKE. N.Y.

FIG. 614 K

Match Box with Cover.

Each........................50c

FIG. 617 K

Match or Soap Box.

Each 30c

FIG. 615 K

Galvanized Iron Manure Can, with Cover.

30 in. high, 24 in. diameter, each. .$12.00

FIG. 616 K

Ornamental Straw Trimming.

For Posts, Floor and Ceiling.

Made from best green cut rye straw; any color braid can be used and made more or less elaborate as may be desired. Floor dressing made any length to match.

Prices given on application.

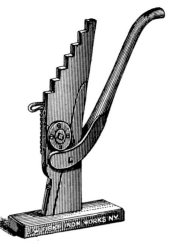

FIG. 618 K

Carriage Jack.

No. 1, each.................$2.50
No. 2, each................. 3.50

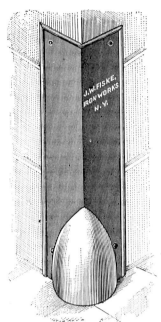

FIG. 619 K

Cast Iron Carriage Wheel Guard.

33 inches high, 7½ inches diameter.

Each.............. $7.00

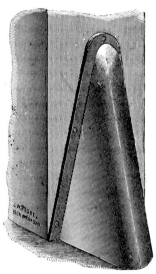

FIG. 620 K

Cast Iron Carriage Wheel Guard.

20½ inches high, 12 inches wide including flanges.

Each..... ....$6.00

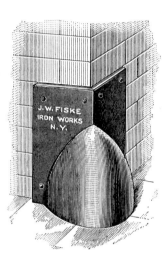

FIG. 621 K

Cast Iron Carriage Wheel Guard.

12½ inches high, 10 inches diameter.

Each $5.00

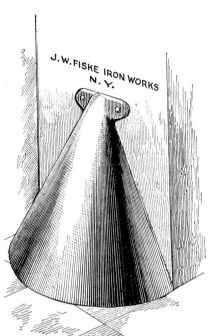

FIG. 622 K

Cast Iron Carriage Wheel Guard.

16 inches high, 22 inches wide.

Each $9.00

FIG. 623 K

Cast Iron Carriage Wheel Guard.

24 inches high, 8½ inches diameter.

Each..................$7.00

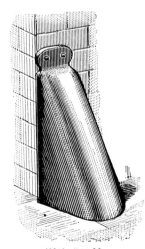

FIG. 624 K

Cast Iron Carriage Wheel Guard.

16 inches high, 6¼ inches wide.

Each............ ....$3.50

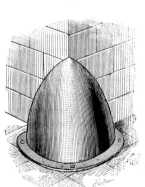

FIG 625 K

Cast Iron Carriage Wheel Guard.

9 inches high, 10½ inches diameter, including bottom flange.

Each.......... ....$3.00

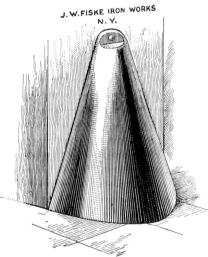

FIG. 626 K

Cast Iron Carriage Wheel Guard.

16 inches high, 13½ inches wide.

Each............................$5.00

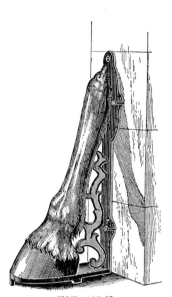

FIG. 627 K

Cast Iron Carriage Wheel Guard.

26 inches high.

Each..... ....$4.00

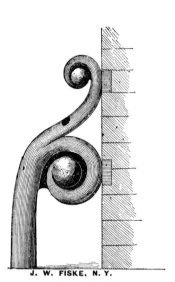

J. W. FISKE, N. Y.

FIG. 628 K

Cast Iron Carriage Wheel Guard.

21 inches high, each....... $5.00

J. W. FISKE, N. Y.

FIG. 629 K

Cast Iron Carriage Wheel Guard.

Each........................$6.00

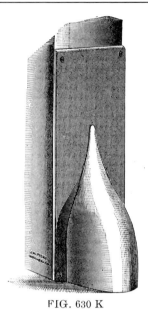

FIG. 630 K

Cast Iron Carriage Wheel Guard.

24 inches high, 6 inches diameter.

Each....................$4.50

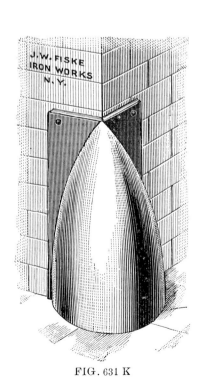

FIG. 631 K

Cast Iron Carriage Wheel Guard.

18 inches high, 12 inches diameter.

Each.......... ....$8.00

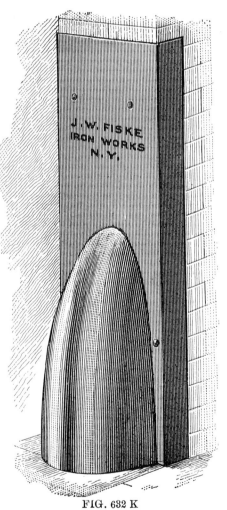

FIG. 632 K

Cast Iron Carriage Wheel Guard.

No. 1, 42 in. high, 16 in. wide, including
flanges, each.....................$17.00

No. 2, 26 in. high, 16 in. wide, including
flanges, each.....................$13.00

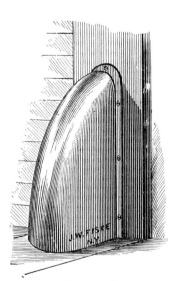

FIG. 633 K

Cast Iron Wheel Guard.

15 inches high, 6 inches wide.

No. 1, Each.........................$2.00

16 inches high, 8 inches wide.

No. 2, Each.........................$2.50

FIG. 634 K
Cast Iron Carriage Wheel Guard.
No. 1, 34 in. high, 15 in. diameter, each.......$21.00
No. 1½, 25 in. high, 15 in. diameter, each...... 18.00
No. 2, 34 in. high, 11 in. diameter, each........ 15.00

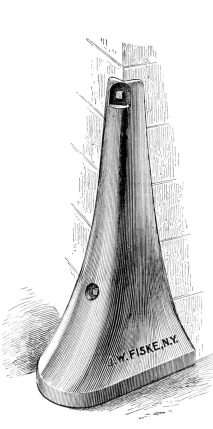

FIG. 635 K
Cast Iron Carriage Wheel Guard.
36 in. high, 14 in. wide, for corner, each $12.00

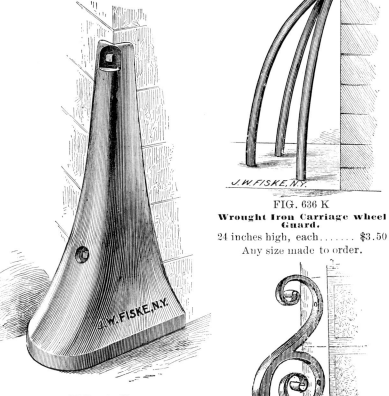

FIG. 636 K
**Wrought Iron Carriage wheel
Guard.**
24 inches high, each...... $3.50
Any size made to order.

FIG. 637 K
**Wrought Iron Carriage wheel
Guard.**
24 inches high, each.........$6.00

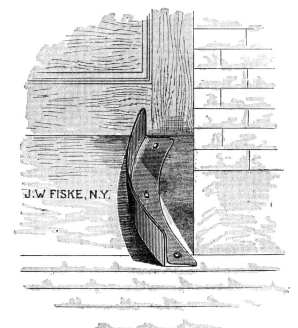

FIG. 638 K
Wrought Iron Carriage Wheel Guard.
To fasten to floor.   Suitable for Fire Engine Houses,
Breweries and Livery Stables.
Price made on application.

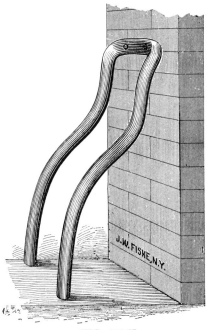

FIG. 639 K
Wrought Iron Carriage Wheel Guard.
24 inches high, 1 inch Iron, each....$2.00
24   "   "   1⅛   "   " 2.50

FIG. 640 K
**Wrought Iron Carriage Wheel
Guard.**
24 inches high, each..........$8.00

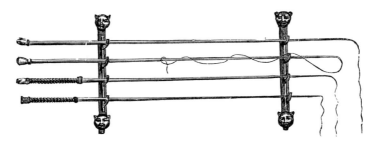

FIG. 641 K

Whip Rack.

Holding 6 whips.

Each...$5.00

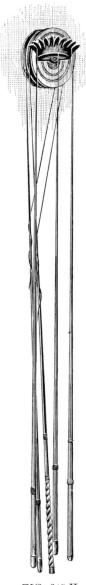

FIG. 642 K

Whip Rack.

Oak or Mahogany Finish

Holding 1 Whip......$ .70
    "   2   "   ..... .85
    "   3   " 1.10
    "   4   " 1.35

FIG. 643 K

Whip Rack.

Brass or Bronze.

Holding 3 Whips, each $6.00

FIG. 644 K

Whip Rack.

Holding

5 Whips, each.......$0.75
Brass................ 3.00

FIG. 645 K

Whip Rack.

Wood, Grooved for 2
Whips.

Projecting Rack, holding
11 Whips.

Each.................$1.00

FIG. 646 K

Whip Rack

Oak or mahogany finish, with brass horse shoe, 6 in. diameter.

For 2 whips......$1.50
" 3 " 1.75
" 4 " 2.00
" 5 " 2.25
" 6 " 2.50

FIG. 647. K

Whip Rack.

Oak or mahogany finish, 6 in. diameter.

For 2 whips......$0.75
" 3 " 1.00
" 4 " 1.25
" 5 " 1.50
" 6 " 1.75

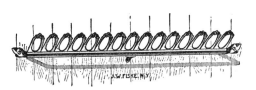

FIG. 648 K

Whip Rack.

Holding 14 whips, each.............$1.50

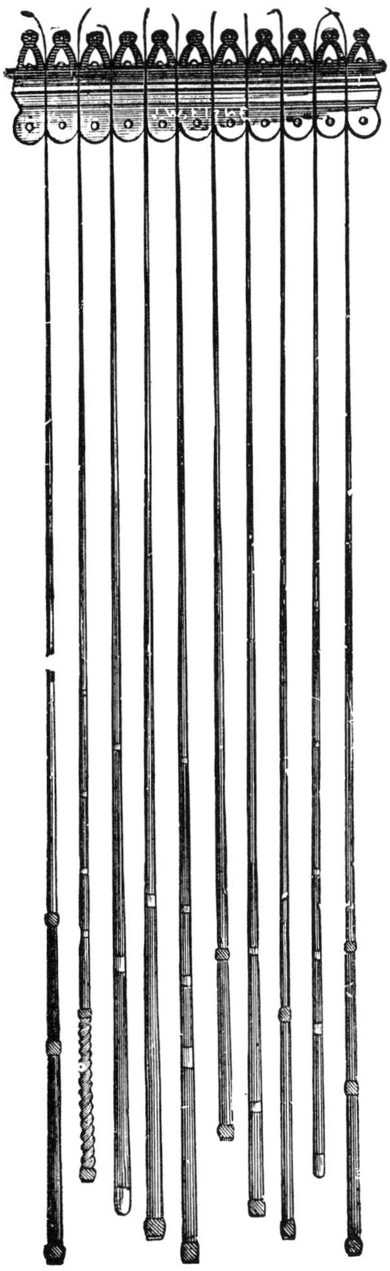

FIG. 649 K

Whip Rack.

BRASS.

Holding 6 whips, each..............$3.50
" 10 " " 4.50

FIG. 650 K

Whip Rack.

Holding 4 whips.

Each,............$5.00

FIG. 651 K

Whip Rack.

Holding 4 whips.

Each.............$3.00

FIG. 652 K

Whip Rack.

BRASS.

Holding 6 whips.

Each............$3.00

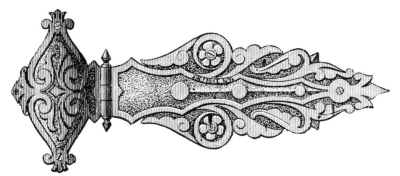

FIG. 653 K

Wrought Iron Box Stall Hinge.

With Ornamental Cast Iron Capping

1 foot 5 inches long from joint to end, Bronzed, per pair............................$7.00
Brass, per pair..32.00

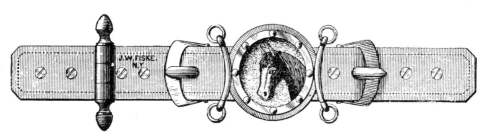

FIG 654 K

Malleable Iron Box Stall Hinge.

Design Patented May, 1885.

2 feet long from joint to end, Bronzed, per pair........ .... $9.00
Brass. per pair...38.00

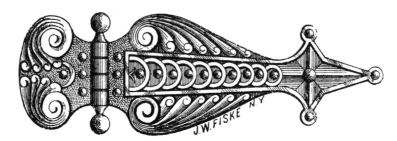

FIG. 655 K

Wrought Iron Box Stall Hinge.

With Ornamental Cast Iron Capping.

1 foot 6 inches long from joint to end, Bronzed, per pair...............................$8 00
Brass, per pair..32.00

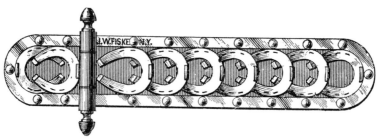

FIG. 656 K

Malleable Iron Box Stall Hinge.

Design patented May, 1885.

1 foot 8 inches long from joint to end, Bronzed, per pair..............................$8.00
Brass, per pair 23.00

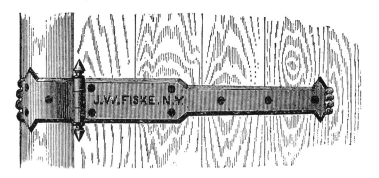

FIG. 657 K

Wrought Iron Box Stall Hinge.

1 foot 6 inches long from joint to end, per pair...$6.00

1 " 6 " " " " " with offset, per pair................................. 7.50

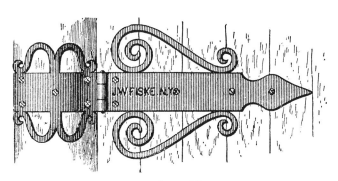

FIG. 658 K

Wrought Iron Box Stall Hinge.

1 foot 2 inches long from joint to end, per pair................................$6.00

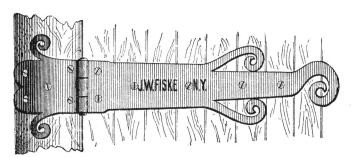

FIG. 659 K

Wrought Iron Box Stall Hinge.

1 foot 7 inches long from joint to end, per pair................................$12.00

FIG. 660 K

Cast Iron Box Stall Hinge.

2 feet 4 inches long from joint to end, per pair.........................$ 7.00

Brass, per pair... 33.00

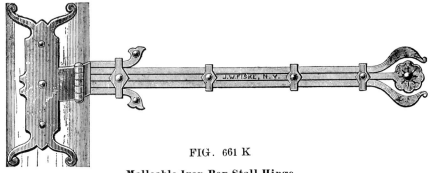

FIG. 661 K

Malleable Iron Box Stall Hinge.

2 feet 4 inches long from joint to end, per-pair...$9.00

FIG. 662 K

Malleable Iron Box Stall Hinge.

2 feet 4 inches long from joint to end. per pair..$8.50

FIG. 663 K

Wrought Iron Box Stall Hinge.

1 foot 6 inches long from joint to end, per pair..$9.00

FIG. 664 K

Wrought Iron Box Stall Hinge.

1 foot 8 inches long from joint to end, per pair..$12.00

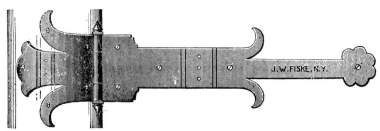

FIG. 665 K

Wrought Iron Box Stall Hinge.

1 foot 8 inches long from joint to end, per pair..$12.00

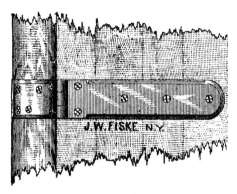

FIG. 666 K

Brass Box Stall Hinge.

No. 1. 1 foot long from joint to end, per pair...$16.50
No. 2. 1 foot 6 inches long from joint to end, per pair.. 17.50

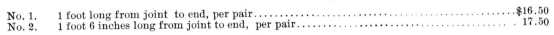

FIG. 667 K

Malleable Iron Box Stall Hinge.

No. 1. 1 foot 10 inches long from joint to end, Bronzed, per pair.................................$ 7.00
No. 2. 2 feet 2   "   "   "   "   " 8.00
No. 1. Brass, per pair....................................... .... 24.00
No. 2.   "   " 30.00

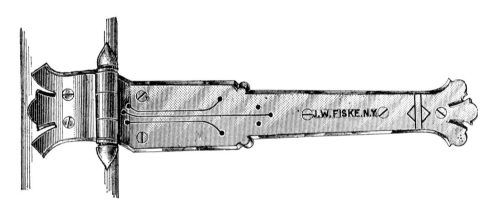

FIG. 668 K

Brass Box Stall Hinge.

1 foot 7 inches long from joint to end, per pair...$25.00

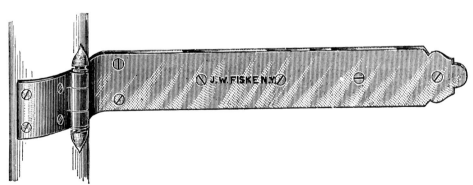

FIG. 669 K

Brass Box Stall Hinge.

1 foot 6 inches long from joint to end, per pair..$27.00

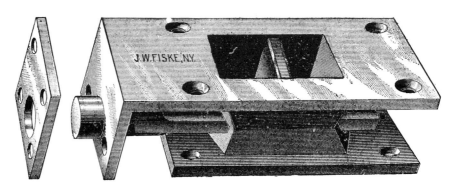

FIG. 670 K

Box Stall Mortice Bolt.

Size, 6 inches long, polished brass, each..................................... ....\$6.00
  " 6   "   Iron, each... .... 1.50

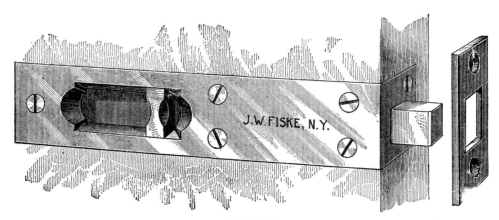

FIG. 671 K

Brass Box Stall Mortice Bolt.

Size, 9 inches long, each.................................... ....\$1.50

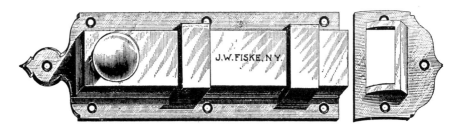

FIG. 672 K

Brass Flush Box Stall Bolt.—Very Heavy.

Size, 8 inches long, each.......................... ... .\$4.00

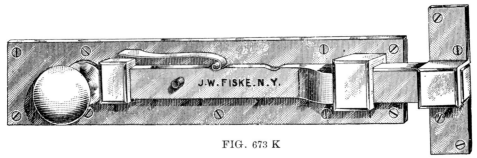

FIG. 673 K

Brass Flush Box Stall Bolt.

Size, 10 inches long, each..... ....\$5.00

FIG. 674 K
Brass Box Stall Latch.

No. 1, with flush drop handle on each side, 3 inches diameter, each.....................................$6.00
No. 2, with flush drop handle on each side, 3½ inches diameter, each..................................... 8.50

In ordering, state thickness of door.

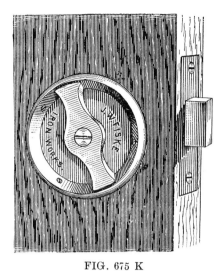

FIG. 675 K
Brass Box Stall Latch.

With flush handle on each side, 2½ inches diameter, each...$4.00

In ordering, state the thickness of door.

FIG. 676 K
Brass Box Stall Latch for Sliding Door.

With flush drop handle on each side, each.....................$9 00

In ordering, state the thickness of door.

FIG. 677 K
Brass Box Stall Lock for Sliding Door.

With flush drop handle on each side, 3 in. diameter, each, $6.00

In ordering, state the thickness of door.

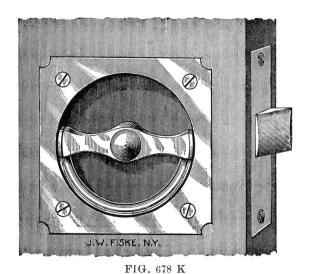

FIG. 678 K

Brass Box Stall Latch.

With flush Drop Handle on each side.

Size of Plates, 4x4 inches, each......................$7.50

In ordering, state the thickness of door.

FIG. 679 K

Brass Box Stall Latch.

With flush Drop Handle on each side.   Extra heavy.

No. 1. 3 x 4 inches, each.......... ....$8.50
No. 2. 3 x 4½ inches, each................................. .... 9.00
No. 3. 3 x 5 inches, each....................................... .... 9.50

FIG. 680 K

Brass Sliding Box Stall Lock.

With flush Handle Plate on each side. Handle also
forming Key for locking door.

Size of Plates, 2¼ x 5½ inches, each $9.00

In ordering, state the thicknes of door.

FIG 681 K

Brass Sliding Box Stall Latch.

With flush Drop Handle on each side.

Size of Plates, 3½ x 5 inches, each.......... . ...$9.00

FIG. 682 K

Door Latch.

12 inches long, malleable iron, each...........$2.50
12 "   "   polished brass,   " 6.00

FIG. 683 K

Door Latch.

12 inch s long, malleable iron, each...........$3.00
12   "   "   polished brass, " 7.00

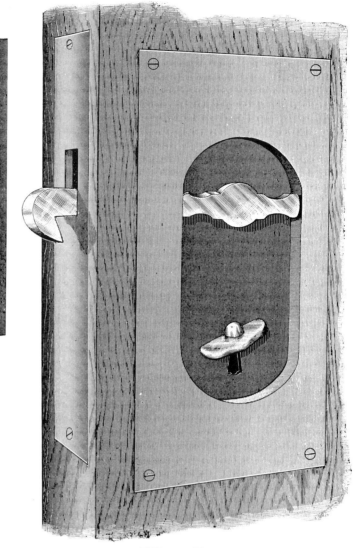

FIG. 685 K
Box Stall Sliding Door Lock.—Extra Heavy.

No. 1. Escutcheon Plate, 3x6 inches, each........................$12.00
No. 2.   "   "   4x8 "   " 18.00

When ordering, give thickness of door and width of stile.

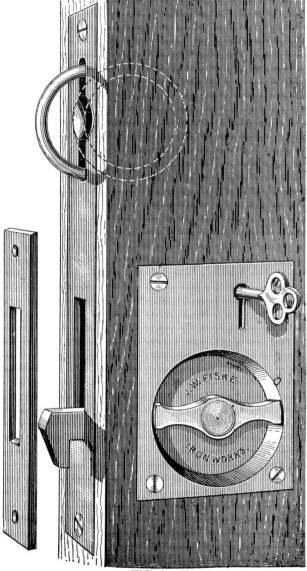

FIG. 684 K
Box Stall Sliding Latch.

With Pull and Cup handle on each side.

With key, each.............$11.00   Without key, each................$10.50

FIG. 686 K
Box Stall Latch.

With flush Drop Handle on each side, with rounded bolt end. Extra Heavy
No. 1. 3 inches diameter, each.$8.50 No. 2. 4 inches diameter, each $9.00

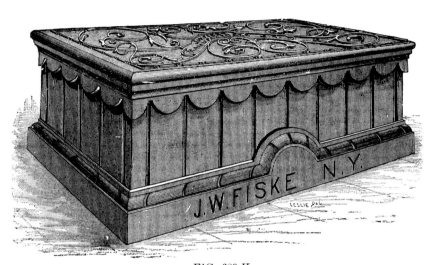

FIG. 689 K

Iron Carriage Stepping Block.

	Painted, one coat	Bronzed
24 inches long, 13 inches wide, 12 inches high, each..... ..	$13.50	$16.00

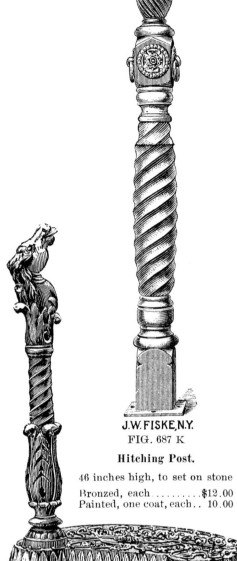

J.W. FISKE, N.Y.
FIG. 687 K

Hitching Post.

46 inches high, to set on stone
Bronzed, each..........$12.00
Painted, one coat, each.. 10.00

FIG. 688 K

Hitching Post and Carriage Step Combined.

	Painted One Coat	Bronzed
To set on stone...........................	$16.00	$20.00
To go into ground.......................	20.00	24.00
Without Hitching Post, to set on stone...	13.50	17.00
" " " to go into ground .	17.50	21.00

FIG. 690 K

Box Stall Latch.

With iron flush Drop Handles and Plates on both
sides.   With brass face latch.

Size of plates, $4\frac{1}{4}$x$4\frac{1}{4}$ inches, each $6.00

HITCHING POSTS.

FIG. 691 K	FIG. 692 K	FIG. 693 K	FIG. 694 K	FIG. 695 K	FIG. 696 K
Horse Head Hitching Post	**Ball Head Hitching Post**	**Pineapple Hitching Post**	**Plain Hitching Post.**	**Whip Hitching Post.**	**Wrought Iron Hitching Post**
43 inches high.	42 inches high.	42 inches high.	42 inches high.	41 inches high.	43 inches high, to set on stone.
Bronzed, each....$8.00	Bronzed, each...$8.00	Bronzed, each...$8.00	Bronzed, each...$6.00	Bronzed, ea..$5.00	Bronzed, each..$16.00
Painted, one coat, each......7.00	Painted, one coat, each.....7.00	Painted, one coat, each.....7.00	Painted, one coat, each.....5.00	Painted, one coat, each..4.00	Painted, one coat, each....14.00

HITCHING POSTS.

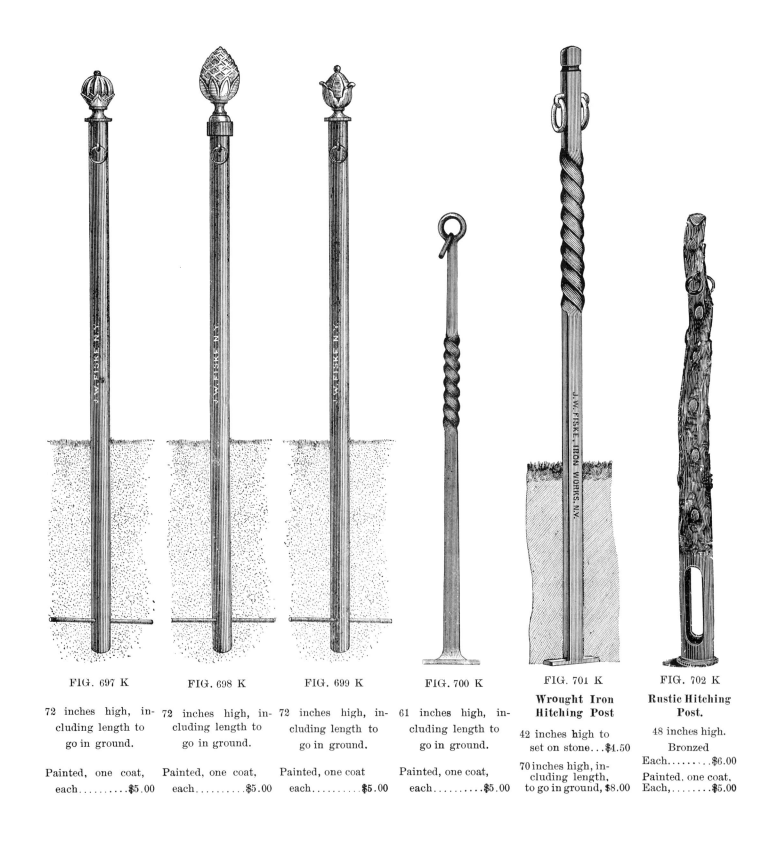

FIG. 697 K

72 inches high, including length to go in ground.

Painted, one coat, each.........$5.00

FIG. 698 K

72 inches high, including length to go in ground.

Painted, one coat, each.........$5.00

FIG. 699 K

72 inches high, including length to go in ground.

Painted, one coat each.........$5.00

FIG. 700 K

61 inches high, including length to go in ground.

Painted, one coat, each.........$5.00

FIG. 701 K

Wrought Iron Hitching Post

42 inches high to set on stone...$4.50

70 inches high, including length, to go in ground, $8.00

FIG. 702 K

Rustic Hitching Post.

48 inches high.
Bronzed
Each........$6.00
Painted, one coat, Each,........$5.00

HITCHING POSTS.

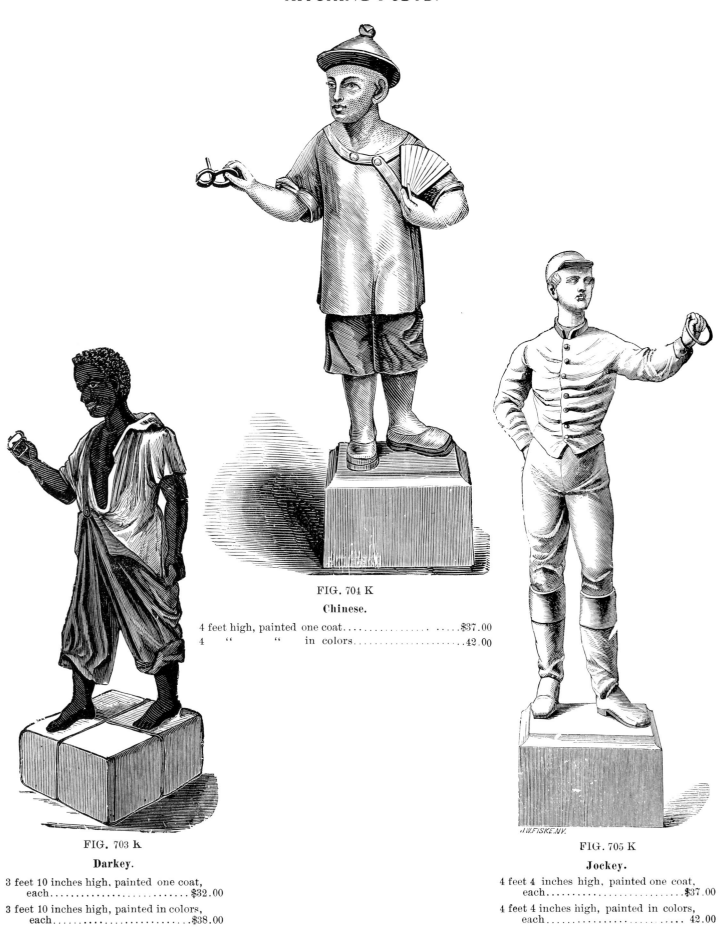

FIG. 704 K

Chinese.

4 feet high, painted one coat................ .....$37.00
4   "   "   in colors.....................42.00

FIG. 703 K

Darkey.

3 feet 10 inches high, painted one coat,
    each............................$32.00

3 feet 10 inches high, painted in colors,
    each............................$38.00

FIG. 705 K

Jockey.

4 feet 4 inches high, painted one coat,
    each............................$37.00

4 feet 4 inches high, painted in colors,
    each........................ ..... 42.00

FIG. 706 K

Bas Relief.—(Zinc.)

1 foot 8 inches diameter, bronzed, each..... ....$45.00

FIG. 707 K

Horse Head.

Beautifully Modeled. Life size—(Zinc.)

One coat of paint, each.......................................$40.00
Bronzed, each 50.00
Gilded with gold leaf, each 60.00
Heroic size, one coat paint, each.... .. ..150.00

The Largest Assortment of Weather Vanes in the United States.

Over 400 Different Designs.

All our Vanes are of Copper and Gilded with Gold Leaf.

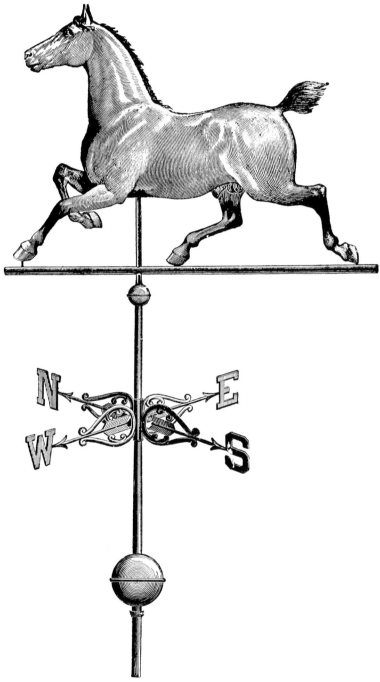

FIG 708 K

Hackney Horse.

No. 1. ¾ Full Bodied, 24 inches long, each...................... $30.00
No. 2. ¾ Full Bodied, 30 inches long, each....................... 50.00
No. 3. ¾ Full Bodied, 48 inches long, each.......................150.00
No. 4. Full bodied, 30 inches long, each...................... 60.00

Separate Illustrated Catalogue of weather vanes furnished upon application.

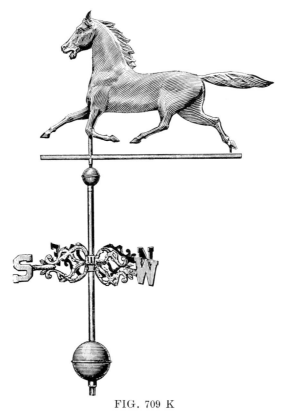

FIG. 709 K

Ethan Allen, Jr.

¾ Full Bodied, 26 inches long, each......... ....$15.00

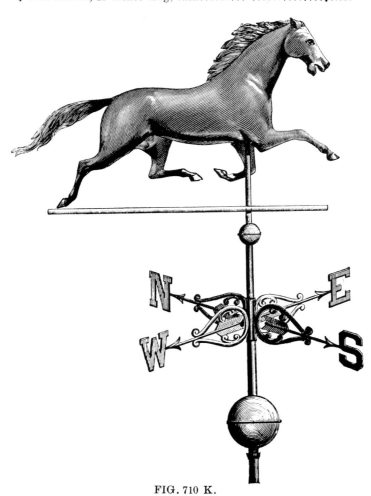

FIG. 710 K.

Ethan Allen.

¾ Full Bodied, 31 inches long, each.......................$20.00

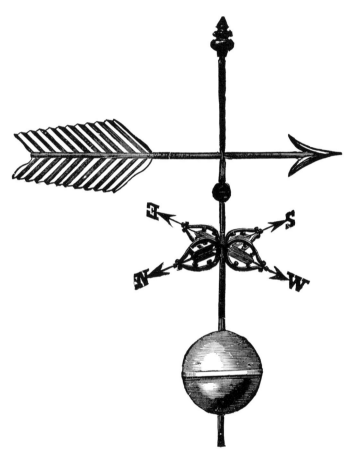

FIG. 711 K

Arrow Vane.

No. 1. 1 foot long, each... $4.00
No. 2. 1 foot 3 inches long, each................................... 5.00
No. 3. 1 foot 6 inches long, each................................... 6.00
No. 4. 2 feet long, each.. 8.00
No. 5. 2 feet 6 inches long, each.................................. 10.00
No. 6. 3 feet long, each... 15.00
No. 7. 3 feet 6 inches long, each.................................. 18.00
No. 8. 4 feet long, each... 20.00
No. 9. 5 feet long, each... 30.00
No. 10. 6 feet long, each... 50.00
No. 11. 7 feet long, each... 70.00
No. 12. 8 feet long, each.. 100.00

Separate catalogue of weather vanes furnished on application.

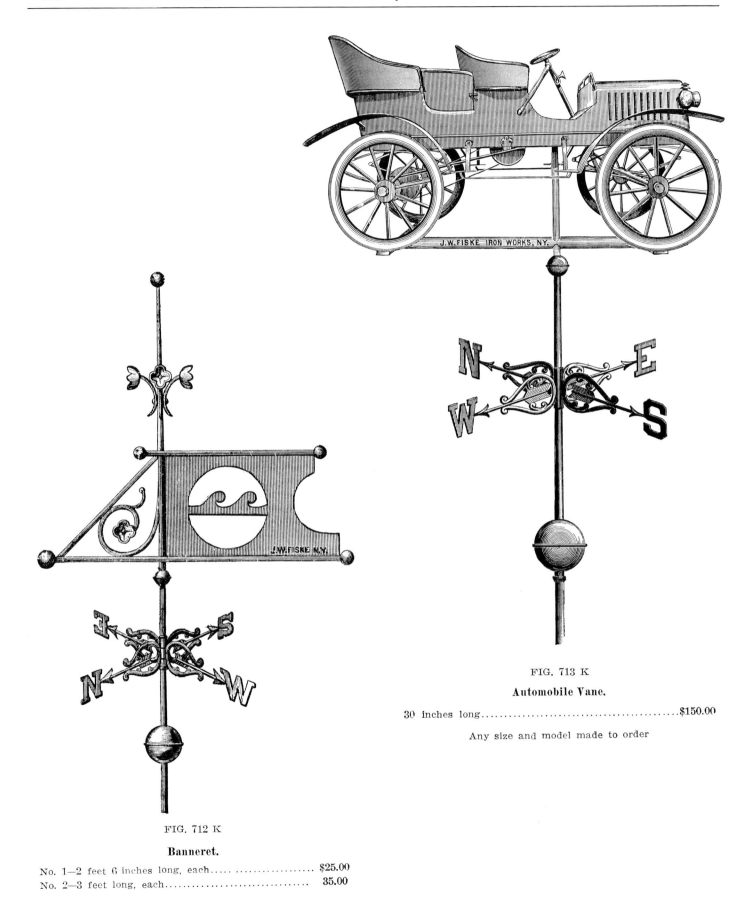

FIG. 712 K

Banneret.

No. 1—2 feet 6 inches long, each..... .... $25.00
No. 2—3 feet long, each............................... 35.00

FIG. 713 K

Automobile Vane.

30 inches long..$150.00

Any size and model made to order

FIG. 714 K

Eagle and Arrow.

No. 1. 6 feet 6 inches..................................$185.00
No. 2. 6 feet.. 170.00
No. 3. 5 feet 6 inches................................. 150.00
No. 4. 5 feet.. 135.00
No. 5. 4 feet.. 70.00
No. 6. 3 feet 6 inches.................................. 50.00
No. 7. 3 feet.. 47.00
No. 8. 2 feet 3 inches.................................. 31.00
No. 9. 1 foot 8 inches.................................. 21.00
No. 10. 1 foot 3 inches.................................. 15.00
No. 11. 0 feet 9 inches.................................. 8.00

FIG. 715 K

Eagle on Ball.

Without arrow. For Flag Pole.

No. A51. 5 feet spread..................................$110.00
No. A52. 4 feet spread.................................. 60.00
No. A52 1-2. 3 feet 6 inches spread..................... 40.00
No. A53. 3 feet 0 inches spread........................ 37.00
No. A54. 2 feet 3 inches spread........................ 29.00
No. A55. 1 foot 8 inches spread........................ 18.50
No. A56. 1 foot 3 inches spread........................ 12.00
No. A56 1-2. 0 feet 9 inches spread..................... 6.00

FIG. 717 K

Flag Pole Ball.

On stem, gilded with best gold leaf.

		Zinc	Copper
No. 226.	3 inches, each	$0.70	$1.00
No. 227.	4 inches, each	1.10	1.50
No. 228.	5 inches, each	1.40	2.50
No. 229.	6 inches, each	2.00	4.00
No. 230.	7 inches, each	3.00	6.00
No. 231.	8 inches, each	3.50	7.50
No. 232.	9 inches, each	6.00	9.00
No. 233.	10 inches, each	7.75	10.00
No. 234.	12 inches, each	12.00	16.00

FIG. 716 K

Rooster.

No. 1—3-4 Full-bodied, 13 inches high.................$ 7.50
No. 2—3-4 Full-bodied, 24 inches high.................. 15.00
No. 3—3-4 Full-bodied, 28 inches high.................. 25.00
No. 4—3-4 Full-bodied, 36 inches high.................. 35.00

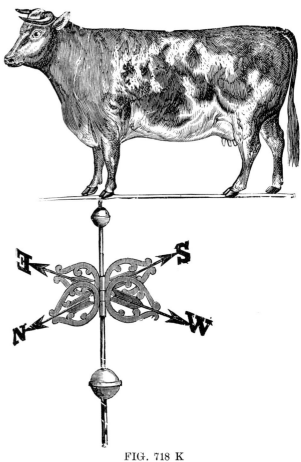

FIG. 718 K

Cow.

No. 1— Full-bodied, 28 inches long..................$40.00
No. 2—3-4 Full-bodied, 28 inches long.................. 30.00
No. 3—1-2 Full-bodied, 24 inches long.................. 20.00
No. 4—1-2 Full-bodied, 28 inches long.................. 22.50

FIG. 719 K

Wrought Iron Guard.

Particularly adapted for filling openings under piazzas, etc.
Made of $\frac{3}{4}$ x $\frac{3}{16}$ iron.

Per square foot...$2.75

FIG. 720 K

Wrought Iron Window Guard.

Rings made of $\frac{3}{4}$ by $\frac{1}{8}$ in. Iron. Scrolls, $\frac{3}{4}$ x $\frac{1}{4}$ in. Iron.

Per square foot................................... $3.25

FIG. 721 K

Wrought Iron Guard.

Particularly adapted for filling openings under piazzas, etc.

Made of $\frac{3}{4}$ x $\frac{3}{16}$ iron. Per square foot..................$2.50

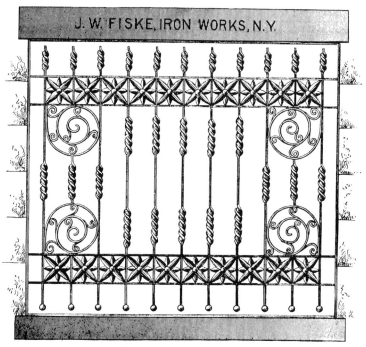

FIG. 722 K

Wrought Iron Window Guard.

Made of $\frac{7}{8}$ x $\frac{1}{4}$ in. Iron.

Per square foot..$2.75

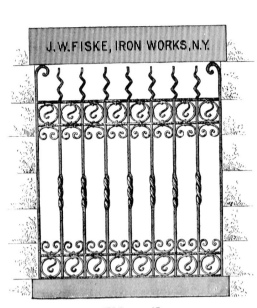

FIG. 723 K

Wrought Iron Window Guard.

Made of ¾ x ¼ iron.

Per square foot.................. ....$2.00

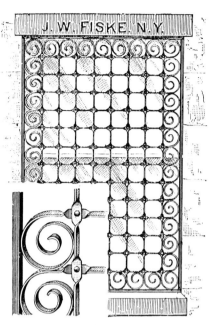

FIG. 724 K

Wrought Iron Window Guard.

Made of 2 inch Mesh ½ x ³⁄₃₂ in. Iron.

Per square foot..................$1.25

Made of 4 in. Mesh, ⅝ x ⅛ in. Iron.

Per square foot..................$1.25

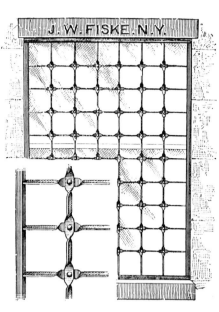

FIG. 725 K

Wrought Iron Window Guard.

Made of 2 inch Mesh, ½ x ³⁄₃₂ in. Iron

Per square foot..................$1.00

Made of 4 in. Mesh, ⅝ x ⅛ in. Iron

Per square foot...............$1.25

FIG. 726 K

Window or Door Guard.

Made of No. 8 Wire, 1½ inch Mesh.

Per square foot................................50c

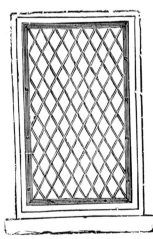

FIG. 727 K

Window or Door Guard.

Made of No. 7 Wire, 2 in. Mesh

Per square foot...........55c

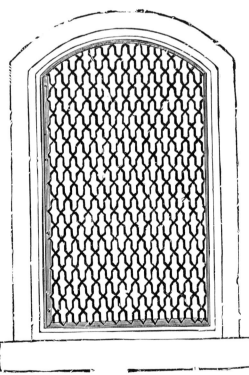

FIG. 728 K

Window or Door Guard.

Made of No. 7 Wire, 3 x 6 inch Mesh.

Per square foot... ....75c

Any size guard and of any size wire and mesh made to order,

FIG. 729 K
Cast Iron Transom Guard.
2 Sizes.
No. 1.   4 feet 1¼ in. wide, 2 feet 1 in. high, each.....$42.00
No. 2.   4 feet ¾ in. wide, 2 feet ¾ in. high, each....... 40.00
Special Designs in Wrought Iron made to order.

FIG. 730 K
Window or Door Guard.
Made of No. 6 Wire.
Per square foot.................................. 90c

FIG. 731 K
Wrought Iron Window or Door Guard.
Made of ½ x ³⁄₃₂ in. Flat Iron, per square foot...........$1.85

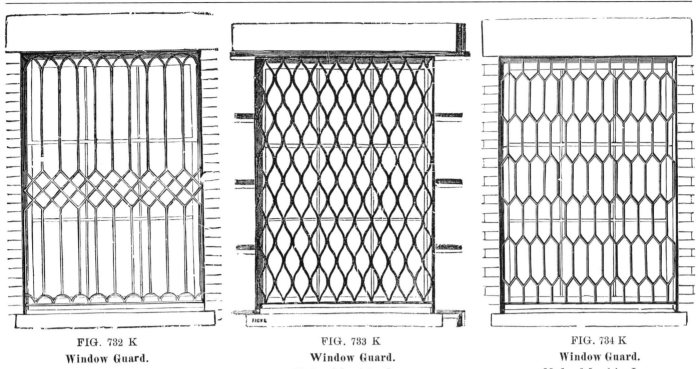

FIG. 732 K
Window Guard.
Made of $\frac{5}{8}$ x $\frac{1}{8}$ in. Iron.
Per square foot................$1.10

FIG. 733 K
Window Guard.
Made of $\frac{5}{8}$ x $\frac{1}{8}$ in. Iron.
Per square foot..................$1.00

FIG. 734 K
Window Guard.
Made of $\frac{5}{8}$ x $\frac{1}{8}$ in. Iron.
Per square foot..................$1.00

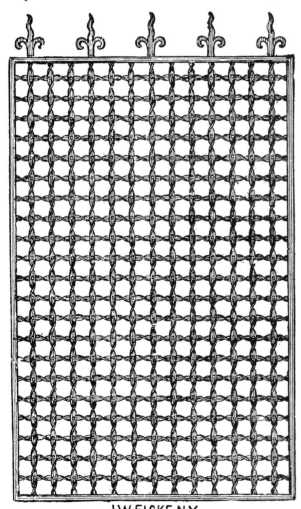

J.W.FISKE.N.Y.
FIG. 735 K
Wrought Iron Window or Door Guard.
Made of $\frac{1}{2}$ x $\frac{3}{32}$ in. Flat Iron.
Per square foot, depending on size of guard....$1.00 to $1.25

J.W.FISKE.N.Y.
FIG. 736 K
Wrought Iron Window or Door Guard.
Made of $\frac{1}{4}$ x $\frac{3}{32}$ in. Flat Iron.
Per square foot, depending on size mesh.........75c to $1.00

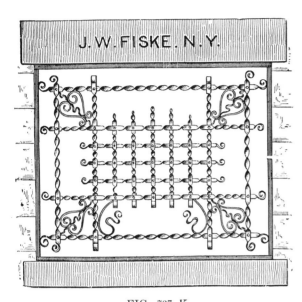

FIG. 737 K

Wrought Iron Window Guard.

Made of $\frac{3}{4}$ x $\frac{1}{4}$ in. Iron.

Per square foot.....................................$1.75

FIG. 738 K

Wrought Iron Window Guard.

Made of 1 x $\frac{1}{4}$ in. Iron.

Per square foot...$2.00

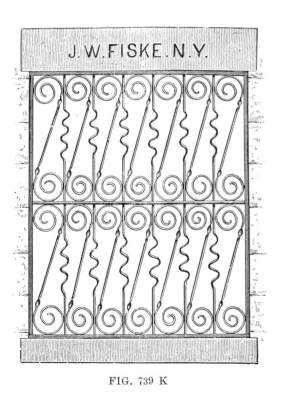

FIG. 739 K

Wrought Iron Window Guard.

Made of $\frac{3}{4}$ x $\frac{1}{4}$ in. Flat Iron, per square foot............$2.00

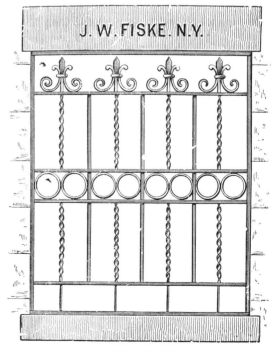

FIG. 740 K

Wrought Iron Window Guard.

Made of $\frac{5}{8}$ x $\frac{1}{4}$ and $\frac{5}{8}$ x $\frac{5}{8}$ in. Iron.

Per square foot.....................................$1.75

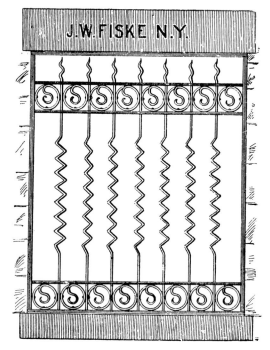

FIG. 741 K

Wrought Iron Window Guard.

Made of ¾ x ¼ in. Iron.

Per square foot....................................$1.80

FIG. 742 K

Wrought Iron Window Guard.

Made of ½ x ¼ in. Iron.

Per square foot....................................$2.00

FIG. 743 K

Wrought Iron Window Guard.

Made of ¾ x ¼ in. Iron.

Per square foot....................................$2.00

FIG. 744 K

Wrought Iron Window Guard.

Made of ¾ x ¼ in. Iron.

Per square foot....................................$2.00

FIG. 745 K

Side Lamp.

For Gas or Kerosene.

Each.
No. 1, 16 in. high, 7x 9 in. wide.....$3.75
No. 2, 18 in. high, 7½x12 in. wide..... 4.50
No. 3, 18 in. high, 10x12 in. wide..... 5.50
No. 4, 22 in. high, 11x16 in. wide..... 7.50

Kerosene Font and Reflector.
$2.25 extra, net.

FIG. 746 K

Triangular Lamp.

For Gas or Kerosene.

Each.
No. 1, 16 in. high, 10 in. wide........$3.25
No. 2, 18 in. high, 12 in. wide........ 3.75
No. 3, 19 in. high, 13 in. wide........ 4.00

Kerosene Font and Reflector,
$2.25 extra, net.

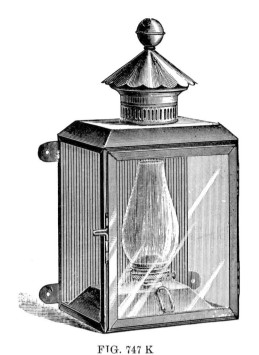

FIG. 747 K

Lamp.

Polished Brass.

For Gas or Kerosene.

Each
No. 1, 17x7½x9½ inches wide............$ 9.00
No. 2, 22x8½x11½ inches wide........ . 11.00

Kerosene Font and Reflector,
$2.25 extra, net.

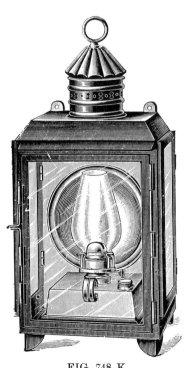

FIG. 748 K

Side Lamp.

For Kerosene.

Each.
20 inches high, 9¼x10½ inches wide... $7.00

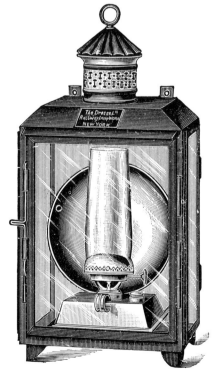

FIG. 749 K

Side Lamp.

For Kerosene.

Each.
23 inches high, 10x12 inches wide... $9.00

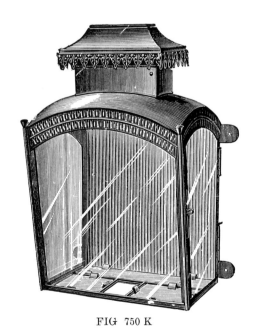

FIG 750 K

Fancy Side Lamp.

Corrugated Silvered Glass Back and Clear
Glass Front.

Each.
24x9x16 in wide, ordinary finish......$10.00
Polished brass finish................. 22.00

Kerosene Font and Reflector,
$2.25 extra, net.

FIG. 751 K

Wrought Iron Lamp and Bracket.

With Bevel Plate Glass.

Lamp 30 in. high, Bracket 9 in. projection to centre of Lamp.

Lamp, alone..........$40.00
Including Wrought Iron
    Bracket........... 50.00

FIG. 752 K

Ornamental Iron Lamp.

With Wrought Iron Base for Gate Posts, etc., with Bevel Plate Glass.
Lamp 24 in. high, Total height 48 inches.

Lamp, alone...............$ 65.00
Including Iron Base......... 115.00

FIG. 753 K
Wrought Iron Lamp and Bracket.
With Bevel Plate Glass.
Lamp 30 in. high, Bracket 24 in. projection to centre of Lamp.

Lamp, alone.......................$ 60.00
Including Wrought Iron Bracket........... 150.00

FIG. 754 K

Wrought Iron Lamp and Bracket.

With Bevel Plate Glass.

Lamp 36 in. high, Bracket 24 in. projection to centre of Lamp.

Lamp, alone... ....$ 70.00
Including Wrought Iron Bracket 105.00

FIG. 755 K
Wrought Iron Lamp and Base.
For Gate Posts, etc., with Bevel Plate Glass. Lamp 30 inches high. Total height 39 inches.
Lamp, alone................................$35.00
Including Iron Base................... 65.00

FIG. 756 K

ILLUSTRATING STABLE FITTINGS
Furnished by J. W. FISKE IRON WORKS
39 and 41 Park Place, New York

STABLE OF
T. N. BARNSDALL,
PITTSBURG, PA.

ARCHITECT,
JOSEPH STILLBURG,
PITTSBURG, PA.

INDEX.